# JUMPSTART TORTS

## Reading and Understanding Tort Cases

# JUMPSTART TORTS

Reading and Understanding
Tort Cases

**ROSS SANDLER**

*Professor of Law*
*New York Law School*

Printed in the United States of America.

5 6 7 8 9 0

ISBN 978-1-4548-0939-5

Sandler, Ross.
    Jumpstart torts : reading and understanding tort cases / Ross Sandler.
        p. cm.
    Includes index.
    ISBN 978-1-4548-0939-5—ISBN 1-4548-0939-6
    1. Torts—United States. I. Title.
    KF1250.Z9S27 2012
    346.7303—dc23
                                                                2011050256

# About Wolters Kluwer Law & Business

Wolters Kluwer Law & Business is a leading global provider of intelligent information and digital solutions for legal and business professionals in key specialty areas, and respected educational resources for professors and law students. Wolters Kluwer Law & Business connects legal and business professionals as well as those in the education market with timely, specialized authoritative content and information-enabled solutions to support success through productivity, accuracy and mobility.

Serving customers worldwide, Wolters Kluwer Law & Business products include those under the Aspen Publishers, CCH, Kluwer Law International, Loislaw, Best Case, ftwilliam.com and MediRegs family of products.

**CCH** products have been a trusted resource since 1913, and are highly regarded resources for legal, securities, antitrust and trade regulation, government contracting, banking, pension, payroll, employment and labor, and healthcare reimbursement and compliance professionals.

**Aspen Publishers** products provide essential information to attorneys, business professionals and law students. Written by preeminent authorities, the product line offers analytical and practical information in a range of specialty practice areas from securities law and intellectual property to mergers and acquisitions and pension/benefits. Aspen's trusted legal education resources provide professors and students with high-quality, up-to-date and effective resources for successful instruction and study in all areas of the law.

**Kluwer Law International** products provide the global business community with reliable international legal information in English. Legal practitioners, corporate counsel and business executives around the world rely on Kluwer Law journals, looseleafs, books, and electronic products for comprehensive information in many areas of international legal practice.

**Loislaw** is a comprehensive online legal research product providing legal content to law firm practitioners of various specializations. Loislaw provides attorneys with the ability to quickly and efficiently find the necessary legal information they need, when and where they need it, by facilitating access to primary law as well as state-specific law, records, forms and treatises.

**Best Case Solutions** is the leading bankruptcy software product to the bankruptcy industry. It provides software and workflow tools to flawlessly streamline petition preparation and the electronic filing process, while timely incorporating ever-changing court requirements.

**ftwilliam.com** offers employee benefits professionals the highest quality plan documents (retirement, welfare and non-qualified) and government forms (5500/PBGC, 1099 and IRS) software at highly competitive prices.

**MediRegs** products provide integrated health care compliance content and software solutions for professionals in healthcare, higher education and life sciences, including professionals in accounting, law and consulting.

Wolters Kluwer Law & Business, a division of Wolters Kluwer, is headquartered in New York. Wolters Kluwer is a market-leading global information services company focused on professionals.

*For Alice Mintzer Sandler,*
*an inspired teacher and editor.*

# Contents

**CHAPTER 6**

# Summary Judgment and Fact Issues

**CHAPTER 12**

# The Finish Line

# Preface

The purpose of *Jumpstart Torts* is to make the student a better lawyer by providing the basic skills to do well in law school.

Students are told to read and analyze judicial opinions to learn the law of torts. But learning torts by reading judicial opinions challenges even the best first-year law students. As one first-year student wrote in an anonymous evaluation "*Jumpstart Torts* makes the study of torts more understandable; it gives a new student a roadmap through an often-confusing terrain." Another first-year student wrote that the "book was helpful in torts, but also for my other courses. It was more useful as an introduction than any of the other school-sponsored materials."

Typical of the difficulties encountered by many law students was the experience of another law student who did not have the benefit of *Jumpstart Torts*:

> I found myself after halfway into my second year of law school and I still did not know what the theory of the case was. The cases in the casebook were very difficult to understand because I did not understand the litigation that was going on. An opinion would discuss the elements of a particular tort, but the reason the judge ruled in favor of either the appellant or appellee would be because of something done procedurally. This was often confusing. The casebooks did not prepare students for the exam.

*Jumpstart Torts* helps a student to become a good lawyer by avoiding such difficulties.

- *Jumpstart Torts* **Introduces the Student to the Language of Law.** Judges use specialty words, unusual definitions, and esoteric phrases. These words and phrases form a barrier to learning. *Jumpstart Torts* defines these terms and explains how they are used in tort cases.
- *Jumpstart Torts* **Explains How to Organize Facts into a Legal Theory.** A lawsuit over an injury begins when the plaintiff's lawyer organizes

the events surrounding the injury into a theory of the case. *Jumpstart Torts* explains how to develop the theory of the case.

- *Jumpstart Torts* **Provides a Formula to Resolve Legal Issues.** Discrete legal issues must be individually identified and analyzed. *Jumpstart Torts* shows how to identify and analyze legal issues.
- *Jumpstart Torts* **Explains Legal Processes and Procedures.** Tort cases are governed by litigation processes and civil procedure. *Jumpstart Torts* explains how the litigation processes and civil procedure apply in tort cases.
- *Jumpstart Torts* **Provides Guidance on Taking a Torts Exam.** Torts students are tested by essay questions where the student must analyze an unfamiliar, complicated fact pattern. *Jumpstart Torts* teaches a successful approach to answering a torts essay question.

*Jumpstart Torts* follows the logic that lawyers use to address actual cases and fact patterns. Chapter 1 defines legal terms and does so in the order that the term would appear in litigation. For example, the term *defendant* follows the term *plaintiff.* This arrangement gives context to the definitions, brings the definitions to life, and encourages comprehension.

Chapter 2 shows how lawyers organize a set of facts into a theory of the case. A theory of the case is the necessary entry point for any legal analysis. By beginning with a theory of the case, the lawyer ensures that the subsequent legal analyses will be relevant.

Chapter 3 provides a basic formula for answering individual, discrete legal questions. The formula is fundamental to legal reasoning and, in combination with the theory of the case, provides a powerful method for understanding and applying tort law.

Additional chapters address such essential litigation concepts as prima facie case, fact issues, motions, presumptions, and the holding of a judicial opinion. Each procedure and concept is illustrated by simple, non-precedent-setting judicial opinions culled mostly from opinions issued by mid-level appellate courts. These brief, mid-level appellate opinions have many advantages for teaching basic lawyer skills. The opinions

- Are short and easy to read
- Deal with ordinary situations, not complex fact patterns
- Apply settled rules of law
- Have memorable and often humorous facts
- Have been made readable by omitting internal citations and procedural histories, and by dividing longer paragraphs into shorter paragraphs
- Use names for easier comprehension rather than such terms as decedent, appellant, plaintiff, and cross-claimant
- Are comprehensible without taking class time

The opinions are all from New York State courts, but this fact is irrelevant to the purposes for which the opinions have been selected. *Jumpstart Torts* addresses basic legal methods, not substantive tort law. The judicial opinions included in *Jumpstart Torts* are meant to complement the substantive material included in any of the many torts casebooks used in law schools across the United States. What *Jumpstart Torts* adds for the student is a road map for doing well in law school and for mastering the lifetime skills required to become a lawyer.

Ross Sandler

# Acknowledgments

I wish to first thank the hundreds of New York Law School students, both day and evening, who inspired me to write *Jumpstart Torts*. This book is, in many ways, a collaborative effort with them. Students submitted excellent comments and suggestions that helped to refine and make more accessible the material in the book.

Professor Michael Sinclair has been particularly helpful in developing *Jumpstart Torts*. He faithfully read and commented on every draft, and, still better, used earlier versions of *Jumpstart Torts* in his tort classes at New York Law School. From these experiences he supplied copious and helpful student notes and comments. Professor David Schoenbrod has also been a regular reader of drafts. He provided many insightful comments and edits as well as excellent advice on law teaching in general.

Many other New York Law School colleagues provided helpful comments and encouragement. These colleagues include Lenni Benson, Anita Bernstein, Carol Buckler, Stephen Ellmann, Aleta Estreicher, Kris Franklin, Cathy Glaser, Lawrence Grosberg, Seth Harris, David Johnson, William LaPiana, Lawrence Levine, Jethro Lieberman, Joseph Marino, Dean Richard Matasar, Michael Perlin, and Sadiq Reza. I thank them for their thoughts and suggestions and for their concern for and contributions to law school teaching.

I especially wish to thank former New York Law School Dean Harry Wellington for encouraging me to teach torts when I first began teaching law. Thanks also to NYU law professor Richard Epstein for allowing me to audit his first-year torts course, and to Yale law professor Peter Schuck for encouraging this project.

*Jumpstart Torts* benefits greatly from the talents of Jeff Hopkins whose drawings liven up the text and bring the judicial opinions to life. My assistant Jennifer Morgan expertly prepared the manuscript and obtained needed permissions.

I would also like to thank my colleagues at the Center for New York City Law, Frank Berlen, Associate Director, and CityLaw Fellows Luna Droubi and Frank St. Jacques, for their helpful assistance in preparing the text for publication.

Richard Mixter of Wolters Kluwer Law & Business deserves special acknowledgment. He spent long hours talking with me about teaching and about how this project might prove useful to a broader segment of students. I am indebted to him for both his insights and encouragement. I am grateful to Barbara Lasoff, Senior Managing Editor, who professionally guided the publication of *Jumpstart Torts* and the *Jumpstart* project. I am also grateful to Sylvia Rebert, Project Manager for Progressive Publishing Alteratives, for expertly managing the production of *Jumpstart Torts*.

My wife, Alice Mintzer Sandler, a former Bank Street teacher, and co-initiator of this project, read and re-read the text for editing, pedagogy and presentation. Her insights into how students learn were indispensable in the design and writing of *Jumpstart Torts*. The book would not have succeeded without her many contributions.

# Legal Terms
## The Players, Actions, Order of Appearance, Settings, and Dramatic Events

T his chapter presents many of the terms, idioms, and procedures encountered in reading judicial opinions in tort cases. The terms are presented in the order that they might appear in a tort litigation. The chapter is not a substitute for the use of a good law dictionary that contains far more entries. There are also many subcategories of these terms as well as technical definitions and usages that would, if included here, make the chapter too long and less useful.

Chapter 1 is designed to be read straight through as a prelude to reading actual court opinions. This format has the advantage of associating terms and events that go together but which would be separated if placed in alphabetical order. Matched pairs like plaintiff and defendant and complaint and answer appear together, while events like depositions and motions for summary judgment are placed in the order in which they appear in litigation.

For ease of locating definitions later, all of the terms are included in the index at the end of the book. Ultimately, all of these terms should be memorized and integrated into your working vocabulary as a lawyer.

## A. BACKGROUND

**Plaintiff:** The injured person who initiates the lawsuit and who is seeking compensation.

**Defendant:** The person against whom the plaintiff has brought a lawsuit and from whom the plaintiff seeks compensation.

**Court:** The location of judicial activity, either trial or appellate. Lawyers also use the term *court* as a synonym for *judge* or *panel of judges*, as in the statement that "The court wrote in its opinion . . ." or "The court decided . . . ."

**Trial Court:** The trial court is where tort cases are initially tried and where fact disputes are resolved by the jury.

**Jury:** The jury resolves factual disputes between the parties, including how much compensation to award the injured party. Juries usually are made up of 6 or 12 persons selected for each case from panels of persons called to jury duty. A trial jury resolves disputes by "finding the facts." The parties to a litigation may waive a jury and instead submit their factual disputes to the trial judge sitting without a jury, in which case the trial judge becomes the fact finder.

**Common Law:** Common law is the legal system that evolved from English judge-made law. The major characteristic of common law is that it developed, and continues to develop, out of judicial decisions in individual cases rather than from statutes enacted by state legislatures. The body of English common law was received by each of the states of the United States, except Louisiana, and continues to form the basis of the law of each state. Because each state has its own version of the common law, tort law may vary from state to state.

**Tort:** The name given to a wrong or wrongful act causing injury, for which a legal claim may be made. *Black's Law Dictionary* defines a tort as "a legal wrong committed upon the person or property independent of contract." The distinction made by this definition is between tort and contract. If a person trips on a hazard in a grocery store and is injured, the wrong is a tort and the claim for compensation is made pursuant to tort law. If, by contrast, the grocery store hired the person but then refused to pay the promised salary, the wrong would be a breach of contract, and the claim for the wrongfully withheld salary would be under contract law.

**Common Law Tort:** A common law tort claim is a claim based on the breach of the common law of the state. A common law tort is distinguished from a statutory tort. A statutory tort is a claim based on the breach of a statute enacted by the state legislature.

**Negligence:** A claim for negligence is a common law claim for compensation for an injury suffered by the plaintiff that was caused by the negligent conduct of the defendant. Negligent conduct is conduct that falls below the standard established by law for the protection of others against unreasonable risk of harm.

**Injury:** Injury is the basis for a claim in tort. A physical injury refers to either bodily injury or property damage. Injuries may also include injuries to emotional well-being, reputation, pain and suffering, medical expenses, and loss of income.

**Damages:** Damages are the monetary compensation sought by the plaintiff to compensate for the injury suffered. The terms *injury* and *damages* are not interchangeable. *Injury* refers to the actual physical or mental harm experienced by the plaintiff, while the term *damages* refers to their monetary equivalent.

**Liability:** The term *liability* refers to the judicial finding that a party is legally answerable to another party. A plaintiff's tort claim for an injury may be divided into two phases: the liability phase and the damages phase. The liability phase determines whether the defendant is legally answerable for the injury. The damages phase determines the amount the defendant must pay the plaintiff in compensation for the injury.

**Evidence:** Evidence consists of those testimonial statements, objects, and documents allowed to be presented in a trial court for consideration by the jury. The rules of evidence govern what testimony or documents may be allowed to be admitted into evidence during the trial. For example, witnesses may be allowed to testify about what they actually saw themselves but may not be allowed to testify about what someone else told them they saw (hearsay).

## B. PRETRIAL PRELIMINARIES

**Lawsuit:** A lawsuit is a commonly used nontechnical term for any civil claim filed in a court of law. A synonym is the word *action*, which is usually defined as a civil law claim brought by one private party against another private party. A criminal charge is referred to as a prosecution rather than a lawsuit.

**Complaint:** The complaint is the initial written document in a civil action that formally sets out the plaintiff's claim against the defendant. In the complaint the plaintiff identifies the defendant or defendants, sets out the facts on which the plaintiff bases his or her theory of the case, and describes the injury and amount of compensation demanded. The part of the complaint in which the plaintiff sets out the monetary demand is sometimes referred to by the Latin phrase, *ad damnun* clause. Some states prohibit plaintiffs in tort cases from stating a dollar amount in the *ad damnun* clause to prevent unrealistic multi-billion dollar claims from being asserted.

**Summons:** A summons is the formal, judicially required notification to the defendant that the plaintiff has commenced an action against the defendant. The nature of the action and facts supporting the action are set out in the complaint, not the summons.

**Claim for Relief or Cause of Action:** These terms refer to the sections of the complaint in which the plaintiff sets out the plaintiff's separate theories supporting compensation. A plaintiff often alleges more than one claim for relief or cause of action. The usual practice is to separate the claims by headings such as First Claim for Relief, Second Claim for Relief, or First Cause of Action, Second Cause of Action, and so forth. Separate claims for relief or causes of action are intended to represent separate theories of the case. The term *cause of action* is sometimes used as a synonym for theory of the case.

**Answer:**  The answer is the defendant's formal written response to the plaintiff's complaint in which the defendant denies or admits the plaintiff's allegations of facts, and asserts any affirmative defenses he or she might have to the plaintiff's claims or causes of action.

**Pleading:**  Pleading is the general term used by the common law to describe the documents bringing an action to court. The pleadings in a case refer to the complaint and answer, as well as other filings with the court setting out a party's formal claims or defenses.

**General Defense:**  In a general defense, defendants deny the truth of, or the legal implications of, the allegations set out by the plaintiff in the complaint.

**Affirmative Defense:**  In an affirmative defense the defendant sets out additional allegations that, if established, would affirmatively refute the plaintiff's claims. An affirmative defense is affirmative in the sense that the defendant bears the affirmative burden to allege and then to prove the defense. Examples of affirmative defenses in a negligence case include the claim that the plaintiff assumed the risk of injury or, by his or her own negligence, caused or contributed to the injury. There also may be procedural affirmative defenses such as lack of jurisdiction over the defendant, or that the plaintiff missed the deadline set by the statute of limitations for filing a complaint.

**Limitations:**  A statute of limitations is a legislative enactment prescribing the time within which a particular type of claim may be enforced in court. A typical statute of limitations for a negligence complaint may require that an action be commenced within three years of the injury.

**Discovery:**  Discovery is the general term for court-sanctioned processes used prior to trial by which each party obtains information about the other side's claims or defenses. The term *discovery* covers a wide variety of methods. These include oral testimony under oath, physical examination by medical experts, written answers to written questions, exchanges of documents, and inspections of articles or locations. Discovery avoids surprises at trial, allows each party to assess the strength or weakness of each other's position, and encourages settlement of the claim prior to trial.

**Deposition:**  A deposition, or an examination before trial, is oral testimony given under oath, usually in a lawyer's office without a judge present. The questioning is done by each party's attorney. An oral deposition is usually transcribed, recorded, or videotaped, and has the effect of locking in a party or witness's story. Under appropriate circumstances, the testimony may be read into evidence at the trial or used to challenge a witness's trial testimony.

**Motions:** Parties to a litigation bring legal issues to the judge for resolution by making a motion. For example, a defendant might move (i.e., ask the judge) to dismiss the plaintiff's complaint, or move to disqualify an expert witness. The correct usage is a party *moved* or *made a motion*, as in the defendant moved for summary judgment; never a party *motioned* the court. Motions may be written or oral, depending on the circumstances. The judge either denies or grants a motion. It is incorrect to say the judge approved, sustained, or adopted a motion.

**Movant and Nonmovant:** The movant is the party making a motion. The nonmovant is the person against whom the motion is made.

**Affidavit:** An affidavit is a formal written statement, made under oath or affirmed, given by either a party or a witness, and used to bring a fact or opinion to the attention of the judge. For example, the defendant in an auto accident lawsuit might submit an affidavit by a witness describing what the witness saw as support for the defendant's motion for summary judgment.

**Motion to Dismiss the Complaint:** A motion to dismiss a complaint is a motion made by a defendant asking the trial judge to rule the plaintiff's complaint deficient as a matter of law.

**Demurrer:** A demurrer is the older common law term for a motion by the defendant to dismiss the complaint as deficient as a matter of law.

**Summary Judgment:** A motion for summary judgment asks the trial judge to decide the case without a trial. The motion may be made by either the plaintiff or defendant. The party making the motion seeks to convince the judge that there is no dispute concerning a material fact, and as a result, there is no need to have a trial to resolve factual disputes. The judgment is "summary" in the sense that it eliminates the fact-finding portion of the trial and allows the judge to decide the case and go straight to the entry of judgment.

**Order:** When a judge directs that something be done or not be done, that directive is called an *order*. An order can be as limited as directing a witness to appear at a deposition to answer questions, or it can affect the entire case as, for example, an order dismissing a plaintiff's complaint.

*Ruling* versus *Finding*: These terms are often confused. The correct usage is that legal issues are ruled upon, and facts are found. The verbs reflect the distinctive roles played by the judge, who rules on the law, and the jury, which finds the facts. Because the roles are not interchangeable, neither are the terms. *Correct*: The judge *ruled* that the complaint stated a cause of action for which relief could be granted, while the jury *found* the defendant was negligent in running the red light.

## C. THE TRIAL

**Burden of Going Forward:** The burden of going forward determines the order in which the trial proceeds. Generally the plaintiff has the burden of going forward first with the plaintiff's direct case. The defendant has the burden of going forward with evidence to support an affirmative defense, but only after the plaintiff has successfully presented the plaintiff's direct case.

**Burden of Persuasion:** The ultimate burden in the litigation is called the burden of persuasion, or, alternatively, the burden of proof. The "burden" in the term is the risk of nonpersuasion. In a tort case the burden of persuasion falls on the plaintiff, who must establish by a preponderance of the evidence all of the elements necessary to sustain his or her claim. The defendant may also have a burden of persuasion when, for example, the defendant asserts an affirmative defense.

**Direct Case:** The direct case is either party's initial presentation of evidence at trial. A direct case is not complete until the opposing side has had an opportunity to cross examine the witnesses presented by the party offering the direct case.

**Prima Facie:** In Latin, the term means "at first sight." A prima facie case is one where the evidence is sufficiently persuasive to establish the fact asserted. A party establishes a prima facie case by producing factual evidence in support of his or her claim which is sufficient to require the opposing party to respond. A plaintiff has presented a prima facie case when it can be said that a jury, after viewing all of the evidence presented by the plaintiff, could decide in favor of the plaintiff's theory of the case. The judge, acting as gatekeeper, decides whether the plaintiff has met the burden of producing a prima facie case.

**Material Fact:** A material fact is a fact that has substantial importance to the result at trial. A material fact possesses the capability of properly influencing the result of the trial.

**Inference:** An inference is a fact not directly proved, but which is logically drawn from another fact or truth. Facts are inferred through a process of reasoning by which the fact or proposition sought to be established is deduced as a logical consequence from other facts already proved or admitted. Inferences may be strong or weak, possible or impossible, compelling or improbable. Much of the art of advocacy involves identifying and evaluating the strengths or weaknesses of inferences.

**Fact Issue and Triable Issue:**  A fact issue is a dispute between the parties over the existence of a fact, the interpretation of a fact, or the inferences that may be drawn from a fact. Fact issues are resolved by the jury or, when there is no jury, by the judge. A triable issue is a fact issue of sufficient materiality that its resolution requires a trial.

**Preponderance of the Evidence:** Preponderance of the evidence is the general standard or measure by which the jury resolves a fact issue in a tort trial. Preponderance of the evidence is usually described as evidence sufficient to make a fact more likely than not. It is not a precise measure. It allows for uncertainty because the conclusion reached by the jury need not be without doubt, only that it is supported by a preponderance of the evidence. This standard is less strict than the well-known beyond a reasonable doubt standard used in a criminal trial.

**Instructions:** At the conclusion of the evidentiary portion of the trial, the judge speaks directly to the jury and instructs the members of the jury on how they are to resolve the fact issues developed in the trial. These instructions may also be referred to as the judge's charge to the jury. Jury instructions are also sometimes given at the beginning of the case.

**Verdict:**  The verdict is the decision by the jury resolving the fact issues, including whether and how much compensation in damages the defendant should pay the plaintiff.

**Motion to Set Aside a Verdict:**  After the jury has returned its verdict, a party may move to set aside the verdict on the grounds that the evidence could not, under any reasonable interpretation, support the verdict. This motion is also called a motion for a judgment n.o.v., an abbreviation of the Latin *non obstante veredicto*. The judge should allow the verdict to stand so long as the jury's verdict may be supported by a reasonable interpretation of the evidence.

**Judgment:**  The judgment is the final order in a tort case that incorporates the jury's verdict and the judge's approval of the verdict. The trial of a case concludes when the trial judge orders that a judgment be entered by the clerk of the court in the court's official records. A judgment is entered irrespective of whether the plaintiff or the defendant wins. As a technical matter, a judgment is usually not final until it is actually entered by the clerk of the court.

**Settlement:**  A settlement is an agreement ending the litigation by consent of the parties. Most tort claims end in a settlement and are not fully tried all the way to a jury verdict. Settlements have the advantage of allowing the parties to agree on the amount of compensation that must be paid rather than have the jury impose an amount.

## D. POST-TRIAL APPEAL

**Appeal:** A litigant on the losing side of a ruling by the trial court judge may appeal to a higher court. Each state has its own rules governing when an appeal might be taken. In some states an appeal may only be taken at the conclusion of the trial after entry of judgment, whereas other states allow appeals to be taken prior to or during the trial. For instance, in some states an appeal may be taken after a judge has denied a party's motion for summary judgment, while other states refuse to allow the losing party on a motion for summary judgment to appeal until the entire trial is over.

**Appellate Court:** An appellate court is a court that hears appeals. Most states have two levels of appellate courts, a mid-level appellate court and a high court.

**Appellant:** The appellant is the party who has appealed. Either plaintiff or defendant may appeal, so either may be called the appellant when he or she gets to the appellate court. Sometimes an appellant is called the petitioner.

**Appellee:** The appellee is the party responding to the appeal. The appellee defends the order or judgment of the trial court which is being challenged by the appellant. Sometimes an appellee is called a *respondent*.

**Appellate Issue:** An appellate issue is the legal question put before the appellate court by the appellant.

**Opinion:** A judicial opinion is a judge's formal explanation, usually written, stating the basis for the judicial decision.

**Holding:** The holding is the appellate court's answer to a legal question. An appellate court affirms, reverses, or modifies the decision from the lower court.

**Remand:** A remand is an order by an appellate court sending the case back to the lower court. A remand may include additional instructions to the lower court judge as set out in the opinion of the appellate court.

## E. HELPFUL TORT TERMS

**Breach:** The term *breach* in a negligence case indicates that the defendant's conduct did not measure up when compared to the appropriate standard of care. Breach is a conclusion rather than a factual allegation. In considering whether a breach has occurred, the jury must compare the defendant's actual conduct with what a person should have done as required by the standard of care.

**Comparative Negligence:** Under a comparative negligence regime (also called comparative fault), the jury allocates responsibility for the injury among the parties. Thus, damages awarded to the plaintiff will be reduced by the percentage of responsibility that the jury assigns to the plaintiff's own conduct. Comparative negligence has the advantage of assuring the plaintiff of some recovery even in circumstances where the plaintiff was partially responsible for his or her own injury. This method of allocating fault replaced the common law rule of contributory negligence under which the plaintiff was denied all compensation if the plaintiff's own negligence contributed to his or her injury. Different versions of comparative negligence exist among the states and vary as to whether and how the calculation is to be made.

**Constructive Knowledge or Constructive Notice:** These terms are synonyms and describe the circumstance where the facts in the case are sufficient for the jury to infer that the person knew or should have known, and therefore that person can be treated as if he or she in fact did know.

**Duty of Care:** To have a duty of care denotes that one person has a legally enforceable obligation to another, the breach of which permits the injured person to be compensated. In a negligence case, duty is a threshold issue to be decided by the judge. Whether there is a duty of care, however, cannot be analyzed without first setting out the theory of the case.

**IRAC:** The acronym IRAC refers to a standard form of legal analysis useful for addressing single, discrete legal issues. The letters stand for Issue, Rule, Analysis, and Conclusion.

**Proximate Cause:** The term *proximate cause* describes judicially created standards to decide how broadly to extend liability for injuries resulting from an individual act of negligence. Application of the doctrine of proximate cause triggers consideration of fairness and foreseeability to limit the rippling effects of negligent conduct. Proximate cause, as a result, is a conclusion following application of the standards rather than an allegation of fact. The *Restatement of Torts (Third)* prefers the term *scope of liability* rather than the term *proximate cause* because the concept is one of limitations of liability rather than factual causation. *Restatement of Torts (Third)* Section 29.

**Res Ipsa Loquitur:** This is a Latin phrase for "the thing speaks for itself." It is used to describe the factual circumstances where the injury could only logically happen as a result of the negligence of the defendant.

**Restatement of Torts:** Because tort law varies from state to state, the American Law Institute, a legal reform organization of lawyers, academics, and judges, publishes a treatise on tort law with the goal of having the states bring their tort laws into greater agreement with each other and to do so by selecting the better of the various state rules available. The treatise presents its conclusions as numbered rules, with explanations and examples. There have been three restatements of torts and a separate restatement of products liability. Judges view the restatements as persuasive but not binding.

**Standard of Care:** The standard of care is the standard against which the defendant's conduct is judged in a negligence case. The general standard of care for common law torts is what a reasonable person would do in the same or similar circumstances. The standard of care may vary as, for example, with respect to physical conditions like blindness, professional activities like medical services, or, in the case of young children, age and experience.

**Theory of the Case:** A theory of the case sweeps together into a single, broad statement the *factual* elements necessary to support the plaintiff's claim. To create a theory of the case, the plaintiff organizes the facts to support each of the elements the plaintiff must prove to establish his or her claim. Sometimes the term *cause of action* is used as a synonym for theory of the case.

# CHAPTER 2

# The Theory of the Case

A legal question appears initially as a jumble of facts, opinions, and inferences scrambled in no particular order; they are like a newly opened 1,000-piece jigsaw puzzle dumped on the dining room table. Putting the jigsaw puzzle back together requires a plan. Similarly, the lawyer needs an organizing plan to resolve a legal question. The theory of the case provides that organizing plan.

## A. THE THEORY OF THE CASE IS THE FIRST STEP IN DEVELOPING A LEGAL CLAIM

The theory of the case sweeps together into a single, comprehensive statement all of the factual elements necessary to support a plaintiff's claim. It is called a theory because it is a statement of what the plaintiff proposes to prove. It is comprehensive because it must include all of the elements needed for the plaintiff to prevail. It is of the case because the facts included may be only those facts that actually occurred during the particular events that led up to the injury.

Here is the formula for the plaintiff's theory of the case in a negligence case:

**The defendant was negligent because:**

(1) The defendant
(2) Did such and such,
(3) Which was negligent [that is, the conduct fell below the standard of care]
(4) And caused
(5) The plaintiff's injury

Each of the five elements has to be in place for the formula to work:

**(1)** *The plaintiff must identify the defendant.* In most cases identification of the defendant is easy. For example, the negligent driver who knocked down the pedestrian is the logical defendant in a pedestrian's lawsuit. But there are other possible defendants. For example, a possible defendant might be an absent owner of the car or the manufacturer who designed the car with inadequate brakes.

**(2)** *The plaintiff must specify the conduct alleged to be negligent.* What did the defendant do that he or she should not have done, or what did the defendant fail to do that he or she should have done? The driver, for example, may have run a red light, ignored a stop sign, or exceeded the speed limit.

**(3)** *The plaintiff must identify the standard against which the conduct is to be measured.* In a negligence case, the default standard of care in the largest number of cases is what a reasonable person would have done in the same or similar circumstances.

**(4)** *The plaintiff must show that the negligent conduct caused the injury.* If the plaintiff claims that the defendant was negligent by running a red light, the plaintiff must also show that running the red light in fact caused the injury.

**(5)** *The plaintiff must have been injured.* The plaintiff's injuries may include mental and psychological injuries as well as physical injuries.

As an example, in a case involving a driver who knocked down a pedestrian, a plaintiff's theory of the case might read as follows:

> The driver was negligent in that he or she drove without proper lookout; the driver's conduct in failing to maintain proper lookout fell below the standard of what a reasonable person would have done while driving a car in the same or similar circumstances; and that negligent conduct caused the pedestrian's injury.

In practice, lawyers shorten this long statement of the theory of the case by saying something like the driver was negligent in that he or she failed to maintain proper lookout. But you should understand that the short statement is code for all of the elements in the basic theory of the case. Those elements are

- Defendant
- Conduct
- Standard of Care
- Causation
- Injury

These five factual elements provide the structure for a lawyer to organize a legal claim and to begin to identify and resolve the relevant legal issues.

## B. DUTY, BREACH, AND PROXIMATE CAUSE FOLLOW FROM THE THEORY OF THE CASE

Duty, breach, and proximate cause are essential conclusions without which a defendant may not be held liable for the tort of negligence. They are not elements of the theory of the case. Lawyers begin with the theory of the case because the theory of the case lays the factual foundation necessary for an analysis of duty, breach, and proximate cause.

Duty is a legal concept signifying that one person had a legally enforceable obligation to avoid the inadvertent injury of another. Only when a duty of care runs from the defendant to the plaintiff may the injured plaintiff successfully sue the defendant for damages. That a duty of care exists, however, is a legal question, not a factual allegation. Because duty is a legal issue, the judge decides whether a duty exists rather than the jury.

Suppose an onlooker failed to rescue a drowning stranger, and the estate of the deceased stranger sued the onlooker. The estate's theory of the case might be that the onlooker was negligent in failing to rescue the drowning stranger, and that that failure caused the stranger to drown. The legal question that emerges from this theory is whether the onlooker had a duty to the drowning stranger. This is a legal question. To decide whether the onlooker had a duty, the judge relies on the facts that make up the theory of the case. If the onlooker were also an employee at the pool where the stranger drowned, the onlooker might well have an enforceable duty to the stranger, but would not have a duty if the onlooker were a person who just happened to be walking by and who might have, but did not, volunteer to rescue the drowning stranger. Duty flows from the facts that make up the plaintiff's theory of the case and, as in this example, is not itself an allegation of fact.

Likewise the term *breach* is not itself an element of the theory of the case. The term *breach* describes a conclusion reached by the fact finder that the defendant's conduct did not measure up to the standard of care. Breach is a judgment about conduct, not the conduct itself. For example, suppose an automobile driver struck a bicycle rider as both passed through an intersection. The injured bicycle rider alleged that the automobile driver was negligent in that the driver did not maintain proper lookout. A jury would compare the driver's actual conduct with the hypothetical conduct of a reasonable driver in the same or similar circumstances. The term *breach* describes the jury's conclusion that the automobile driver's conduct did fall below the standard of care.

Proximate cause is also a conclusion, not a factual element of the theory of the case. Proximate cause is a judicially created standard that limits the breadth and extent of liability. Courts adopted the proximate cause standard to prevent the rippling effects of negligent conduct from extending liability for an injury beyond the bounds of fairness and foreseeability. For example, suppose that a drugstore clerk heard the bicycle/car accident described in the paragraph above. The clerk ran out of the drugstore to help, and as he ran, he tripped and sprained his ankle. A customer in the drugstore was left without service and was, as a result, late to work. Because the customer was late to work, the customer's company lost a sale. Should the driver who negligently knocked down the bicycle rider also be liable for the clerk's injury, the customer's late return to work, or the loss of the customer's company's sale? Because proximate cause depends on the facts of the theory of the case, a finding of proximate cause also follows the theory of the case.

## C. THE THEORY OF THE CASE ORGANIZES A NARRATIVE OF EVENTS INTO A LEGAL CLAIM

**CASE 1. The snow tuber's dismount: The facts may suggest several theories of the case.** In this case a 16-year-old boy broke his hip while snow tubing at a ski resort. As the boy dismounted his snow tube at the end of the run, another snow tuber ran into him and knocked him over, causing his injury. The boy sued the owner of the ski resort, claiming that the ski resort was at fault for his injury.

THE SNOW TUBER'S DISMOUNT

Because people often injure themselves while participating in sports, the law of torts includes the principle that a person who plays a sport assumes the risks generally associated with that sport. For example, when a person ice skates, he or she assumes the risk of falling. This legal principle of no duty with respect to the ordinary risks of sports presented a challenge for the snow tuber's lawyer. The lawyer for the snow tuber had to organize the facts into a theory of the case which would allow recovery. The theory the lawyer came up with was that the ski resort's employees' actions increased the risk of injury beyond the ordinary risks of snow tubing.

## CORY HUNEAU, plaintiff, v. MAPLE SKI RIDGE, INC., defendant.
794 N.Y.Supp.2d 460 (3rd Dep't 2005)

**The Court:** In March 2001, then 16-year-old plaintiff Cory Huneau was snow tubing with friends at Maple Ski Ridge in the City of Schenectady, New York, when he was struck by other tubers while allegedly attempting to exit after a ride down the hill. He sustained a fractured hip, and he and his parents subsequently commenced this negligence action against defendant Maple Ski Ridge.

Maple Ski Ridge argues that the accident in which Cory Huneau was injured fell within the risks assumed by participating in snow tubing. A person who elects to engage in a sport or recreational activity consents to those commonly appreciated risks that are inherent in and arise out of the nature of the sport generally and flow from such participation. A participant does not, however, assume risks that result in a dangerous condition over and above the usual dangers inherent in the activity.

Maple Ski Ridge's manager acknowledged at her deposition that the duties of the attendant stationed at the top of the run included maintaining a sufficient distance between tubers to afford adequate time to clear the bottom of the run before the next tuber arrived. The attendant at the bottom is supposed to make sure that the exit area is cleared. While Maple Ski Ridge submitted an affidavit from a nonparty witness who essentially stated that the accident occurred because of Cory Huneau's horseplay, Huneau set forth a different version of events.

Huneau testified at his deposition that, without any request by him, the attendant at the summit spun his tube as he pushed him. In his affidavit in opposition to Maple Ski Ridge's motion, Huneau added that the spinning caused him to experience some dizziness, slowing his ability to exit after his ride. He stated that at the end of his ride he bumped into a rider who had not yet cleared the area, causing her to fall. As he then allegedly attempted to clear the area, he reportedly saw two tubers immediately upon him. He claims he tried to jump over the tubers to avoid a collision, but was struck and injured.

We agree with the trial court that, viewing this evidence in the light most favorable to nonmovant, here to Huneau, summary judgment is inappropriate because there are factual issues as to whether the alleged actions of the attendants were inconsistent with their job duties and unreasonably increased the risk of injury.

[The appellate court sent the case back to the trial court for a trial.]

## ANALYSIS

The lawyer for plaintiff Cory Huneau organized the facts that could be directly proved into several different theories of the case against Maple Ski Ridge. The lawyer alleged that, by virtue of its employees' actions, Maple Ski Ridge should be held liable for Cory Huneau's injury because those employees were negligent in that

- They gave Huneau an unwanted spin that made him dizzy.
- They failed to maintain a safe distance between snow tubers.
- They failed to make sure the area at the bottom of the run was clear of snow tubers before the next tuber arrived.

Each theory identified the defendant, the conduct, and the standard of care and showed causation.

Are there other possible theories of the case? Cory Huneau might have alleged other theories, depending on whether there were any supporting facts, such as:

- The defendant Maple Ski Ridge was negligent in that it operated on a day that was too icy for recreational snow tubing, and the icy conditions caused Cory Huneau's injuries.
- The defendant Maple Ski Ridge was negligent in that it had not adequately trained its employees on the procedures needed to prevent injuries to customers while snow tubing, and the inadequately trained employees caused Cory Huneau's injuries.
- The defendant Maple Ski Ridge was negligent in that the design of the get-off area was too small for a safe exit, and the unsafe design caused Cory Huneau's injuries.

A plaintiff's lawyer will develop as many separate, narrow theories of the case as the facts will support. In this way the lawyer makes precise the basis for the plaintiff's claim and maximizes the plaintiff's chances of winning the lawsuit. It is quite possible that the jury in Cory Huneau's case might decide that spinning him at the top of the run was not negligent at all, because being spun by the attendant is an anticipated part of the fun of snow tubing. On the other hand, the jury might at the same time find that not providing adequate supervision for the exit area was negligent because it subjected all snow tubers to unnecessary risks of injury.

It is not necessary to win on every theory of the case, but it is necessary for the plaintiff's lawyer to consider every reasonable theory that the facts will support.

## D. EVERY ELEMENT OF THE THEORY OF THE CASE MUST BE SUPPORTED BY EVIDENCE FOR THE THEORY OF THE CASE TO BE VIABLE

A theory of the case is a chain made up of elements. Some of the elements may be directly proved, like the identity of the defendant or the nature of the plaintiff's injury. Others may require a drawing of the inference, like whether a particular act of the defendant was a "substantial cause" of the injury. If a factual element is missing or unproved, the theory fails.

**CASE 2. The drunk who choked on a hot roast beef sandwich: Sometimes no theory of the case is viable.** In this case a man who got drunk at the local bar subsequently choked to death in a nearby diner while eating a hot roast beef sandwich. His estate sued the MJM Diner that had served the hot roast beef sandwich on which he choked.

A hot roast beef sandwich is not ordinarily thought of as an instrument of danger. The dead man's relatives nonetheless argued, as their first theory of the case, that it was negligent to serve a hot roast beef sandwich to a man who was visibly drunk.

The Diner also failed to post a sign describing the Heimlich maneuver, the widely recognized method to dislodge food from a choking person's throat by a vigorous compression of the victim's solar plexus. The estate, as plaintiff, alleged that the absence of the Heimlich maneuver instruction poster, a violation of state law, was a cause of the drunk man's death.

THE DRUNK WHO CHOKED ON A HOT ROAST BEEF SANDWICH

The trial court ruled that the plaintiff had alleged adequate theories of the case. The diner, the defendant, appealed to a higher court. There the diner got a more favorable result.

**MARGARET FILIBERTO, AS ADMINISTRATOR OF THE ESTATE OF THOMAS R. FILIBERTO,** plaintiff, v. **HERK'S TAVERN, INC. AND MJM DINER,** defendants.
686 N.Y.Supp.2d 886 (3rd Dep't 1999)

**The Court:** Thomas R. Filiberto spent the early morning hours of December 27, 1991, consuming alcoholic beverages at Herk's Tavern located in the City of Amsterdam, Montgomery County, New York.

When the tavern closed at 4:00 A.M., defendant Philip R. Bracchi, the tavern's proprietor, drove Thomas Filiberto to the MJM Diner to eat. A waitress served the men two hot roast beef sandwiches and green beans, and while Filiberto was consuming his food, he stopped breathing. Two patrons of the diner unsuccessfully attempted to execute the Heimlich maneuver on Filiberto, and an employee of the diner telephoned immediately for an ambulance. Filiberto was taken to the hospital where he died.

The wrongful death action was commenced by Margaret Filiberto, on behalf of Thomas, against MJM Diner Inc., contending that MJM was negligent for having served Thomas Filiberto food while he was visibly intoxicated and for the improper placement of the poster with instructions regarding choking emergencies.

MJM moved for summary judgment dismissing the complaint, which was denied by the trial court. MJM now appeals.

Margaret Filiberto asks this court to impose a common-law duty on MJM, a food-service establishment that does not serve alcoholic beverages, to refuse to serve food to a patron who appears to be in an intoxicated condition. While a restaurant has a duty to undertake reasonable care to protect patrons on its premises, a defendant owes no duty to protect a person from the consequences of his or her own voluntary intoxication.

Upon our review of the record, we conclude, as a matter of law, that it was not reasonably foreseeable that Thomas Filiberto would stop breathing or choke as a result of being served a hot roast beef sandwich.

Even viewing the evidence in a light most favorable to Margaret Filiberto, as the court must in a motion for summary judgment, she offered no viable evidence tending to suggest that serving food to an intoxicated person was dangerous or created a foreseeable health risk; the fact that Thomas Filiberto unfortunately died, allegedly as a result of a blockage in his trachea, is not sufficient.

We reject Margaret Filiberto's claim that liability is derived from MJM's alleged failure to place a first-aid poster in a proper location in the diner as required by the New York State Public Health Law. Without addressing whether the placement of the emergency instructions was proper pursuant to law, we find that the location of the poster was not a substantial factor in Thomas Filiberto's death.

The record is clear that immediately after Thomas Filiberto stopped breathing, two patrons came to his assistance. The first patron who attempted to clear the obstruction was a retired firefighter with substantial experience in first aid and the Heimlich maneuver. The second patron, a restaurant manager who was familiar with the Heimlich maneuver, also performed the procedure numerous times. Margaret Filiberto has failed to submit admissible evidence supporting the allegation that appropriate first aid was not provided or that the Heimlich maneuver was not properly administered immediately by two patrons and emergency telephone calls were placed by an MJM employee. Unfortunately, the emergency medical technicians who responded were unsuccessful in removing the blockage. Under these circumstances, we determine that as a matter of law the placement of the poster was not a proximate cause of decedent's death.

### ANALYSIS

The appellate judge rejected Margaret Filiberto's two theories because each theory lacked an essential element.

In serving the hot roast beef sandwich, the court ruled that the MJM Diner did not do anything that was wrong. Filiberto, the court ruled, had not cited any conduct by MJM Diner in serving the hot roast beef sandwich which a jury could reasonably find to be negligent. The Diner's conduct in serving the sandwich may have caused injury, but the element of negligence was missing.

In its failure to post a Heimlich maneuver sign in violation of the state law, the MJM Diner did do something that was wrong. But the element of causation was missing. Not having the sign up did not cause Filiberto's injury.

The estate's lawyer tried, but sometimes there simply are no credible theories to allege.

## E. THE THEORY OF THE CASE APPLIES TO ALL TORTS

*Jumpstart Torts*, for simplicity, uses as examples only negligence cases, but the need to establish a theory of the case is just as compelling for other torts such as intentional torts and products liability. A theory of the case organizes the facts preparatory to the actual legal analysis. Because various types of torts require different factual elements, the theories will also vary. Creating a theory as the initial organizing method, however, remains the same.

For example, battery, an intentional tort, requires at the minimum proof that the defendant intentionally caused harmful or offensive contact to another. Thus the minimum elements of a theory in a battery case would read as follows:

(1) The defendant
(2) Intentionally caused

(3) Harmful or offensive

(4) Contact with another

A theory of the case that could satisfy these minimum elements would have to first identify the defendant and then specify the conduct from which the jury might conclude that the defendant acted intentionally. Intent is a mental state that cannot be proved directly; it must be inferred from conduct. Paraphrasing Justice Oliver Wendell Holmes, even a dog can tell the difference between someone tripping over a dog and someone kicking a dog. An adequate theory would have to identify the conduct from which the inference of intent might be drawn.

A battery claim would also have to include facts to support the conclusion that the contact was harmful or offensive. Proof of harm or offensive contact is easy with a punch in the nose, but not so easy with arguably friendly contact like a kiss, a pat on the back, or blowing smoke in the face of another person.

For products liability, a strict liability tort, a plaintiff at a minimum would have to allege that the defendant was a seller of a defective product, and that it was that defect in the product that caused the plaintiff's injury. The minimum elements of a theory in a products liability case would read as follows:

(1) The defendant is a seller

(2) Of a product

(3) That was defective

(4) And that defect caused the plaintiff's injury

A theory of the case that could satisfy these minimum elements would have to identify the defendant, which is not always easy when the defendant is a distant manufacturer with whom the consumer had no contact. Assuming the seller of the product can be identified, the plaintiff must show that the product in question was defective and that it was the defect that caused the plaintiff's injury.

A theory of the case opens the way for a systematic analysis of relevant legal issues. For example, could a seller of used goods be held strictly liable? Perhaps a seller who also reconditioned a used factory machine might be liable, but not an auctioneer who auctioned the remnants of a decedent's estate on an "as is" basis. Would a defect in the color of a product be sufficient to establish liability? Perhaps not for a manufacturer of a yellow pencil that came out blue, but perhaps liability would be imposed on a seller of a personal life preserver, the defective color of which failed to attract the attention of a search party.

Setting out a theory of the case, regardless of the tort, gets the lawyer off in the right direction.

# CHAPTER 3

# Analyzing the Theory of the Case
## The IRAC Formula

The theory of the case organizes the plaintiff's case so that it may be analyzed. The IRAC formula is one of the methods for analyzing the theory of the case. The theory of the case and the IRAC formula work together in building a competent legal argument, but they perform dramatically different functions. The theory of the case operates at the macro level, while the IRAC formula operates at the micro level. Many students fail to distinguish between the two functions, but the two functions are quite distinct.

The theory of the case operates at the macro level because it sums up the plaintiff's entire factual case. IRAC, on the other hand, works at the micro level. It is a formula for presenting the legal arguments designed to answer single, discrete legal questions. Within any theory of the case, there will be many discrete legal questions or issues. The IRAC formula provides a logical analytical outline for answering these questions.

The acronym "IRAC" stands for the following:

Issue—The issue is a statement of a legal or factual question that requires an answer.

Rule—The legal rule is a statement of the legal rule, standard, or principle that a lawyer would invoke to resolve (answer) the legal issue presented.

Analysis—The analysis is the lawyer's discussion of the facts of the case with the objective of showing how the rule applies to the case being analyzed.

Conclusion—The legal conclusion is the answer to the question presented as supported by the preceding analysis.

The IRAC formula works only with individual, thinly sliced legal issues. It is not appropriate for the outline of an entire cause of action. The distinction between the theory of the case and the IRAC formula might be viewed in terms of a computer screen. The theory of the case is like a home page that lists all of the main elements of a Web site. Individual legal issues are like drop-down menus. The IRAC formula only comes into play to analyze the drop-down individual legal issues.

The term *IRAC* could be misleading, however, because the "R" in IRAC is too narrow a reference. The "R" in most analyses involving torts is really a standard or a principle, not a rule. The formula could just as well have been written "ISAC" for standard, or "IPAC" for principle. Why is this important? It is important because analyses vary greatly depending on whether the lawyer is applying a rule, a standard, or a principle, and in many cases all three are in play.

A rule hinges on one or two facts, and all other facts are irrelevant. A rule produces an inevitable result based on the existence or nonexistence of a particular fact. In many states it is a rule, for example, that a complaint for negligence must be filed within three years from the date the cause of action arose, generally the date of the injury. For such a rule, the only facts that matter are the date the cause of action arose and the date the complaint was filed. All other facts about the injury are irrelevant and immaterial.

A standard is different. A standard allows for the discussion of unlimited facts, with none being determinative. For example, the standard for reasonable care is what a reasonable person would do under the same or similar circumstances. The nature of such a standard is to make relevant every fact concerning the circumstances of the injury. No one fact is determinative. The goal of the analysis from the plaintiff's perspective is to arrange the facts so that they will support the inference that the defendant's conduct fell below the standard of what a reasonable person would have done in the same or similar circumstances. The defendant arranges the facts to reach an opposite conclusion. An analysis based on the standard of reasonable care, while very broad, is still limited to the actual facts of that case. If the day were dry, the plaintiff cannot argue that it was rainy.

A principle is different still. A principle implies a value or a goal. A principle that is often repeated in modern products liability litigation is that it is unfair for a few injured consumers to bear the entire economic burden of their injuries; rather the economic burden of the injuries should be spread throughout the industry. This principle presents a societal value that colors legal arguments. The principle provides a general goal but does not arise out of the facts of the case itself. An argument based on principle is, as a result, not tethered to the facts of the case but allows for a broader discussion of values and goals.

IRAC, as a result, is hardly an automatic exercise. It takes skill to develop the relevant arguments based on rules, standards, and principles. IRAC as a formula, even with these caveats, however, provides an orderly way to approach a discrete legal issue. For the beginner, IRAC provides a road map, a framework, a starting point. By starting with IRAC the student is at least set in the right direction.

## A. THE THEORY OF THE CASE AND THE IRAC FORMULA WORK TOGETHER

As an example, take the Snow Tuber's Dismount, the first case in *Jumpstart Torts, Cory Huneau v. Maple Ski Ridge, Inc.* (See page 15.) One of Huneau's broad, macro theories of the case might be stated as follows:

### The defendant
(1) Maple Ski Ridge, Inc. was (2) negligent in that the staff of Maple Ski Ridge, Inc., failed to maintain an adequate separation between tubers, and it was the (3) inadequate separation between tubers that caused (4) plaintiff Huneau's injury. Under this theory, Maple Ski Ridge, Inc. had a (5) duty of care to plaintiff Huneau. [For convenience, each element has been separately numbered.]

This theory of the case broadly includes all of the elements Huneau needs to prove to establish a prima facie case against Maple Ski Ridge, Inc. Each element, however, requires a separate analysis and separate proof. Using the IRAC formula, it is possible to set up a legal analysis of each of the five key issues raised by this theory of the case.

## 1. FIRST ELEMENT OF HUNEAU'S THEORY OF THE CASE— CORPORATE LIABILITY

**Issue:** Should the defendant Maple Ski Ridge, Inc., a corporation, be held liable?

**Rule:** A corporation is vicariously liable for the torts of its employees acting within the scope of their employment.

**Analysis:** In this section show that Huneau could establish by a preponderance of the evidence that Huneau's injury occurred while the Maple Ski Ridge employees were acting within the scope of their employment.

**Conclusion:** Maple Ski Ridge, Inc., should [or should not] be held liable.

## 2. SECOND ELEMENT OF HUNEAU'S THEORY OF THE CASE— NEGLIGENCE

**Issue:** Were the employees of Maple Ski Ridge negligent?

**Rule:** The conduct of the Maple Ski Ridge employees should be judged against the standard of what a reasonable person would do in the same or similar circumstances.

**Analysis:** In this section show that Huneau could establish by a preponderance of the evidence that the Maple Ski Ridge employees were negligent.

**Conclusion:** A jury could [or could not] find the conduct of the employees negligent.

### 3. THIRD ELEMENT OF HUNEAU'S THEORY OF THE CASE— CAUSATION

**Issue:** Did the negligence of the employees of Maple Ski Ridge cause Huneau's injury?

**Rule:** To be held liable to Huneau, the negligence of the employees of Maple Ski Ridge must have been a substantial cause of Huneau's injury.

**Analysis:** In this section show that Huneau could establish by a preponderance of the evidence that the negligence of the employees of Maple Ski Ridge was a substantial cause of his injury.

**Conclusion:** A jury could [or could not] find that the negligence of the employees of Maple Ski Ridge was a substantial cause of Huneau's injury.

### 4. FOURTH ELEMENT OF HUNEAU'S THEORY OF THE CASE— INJURY

**Issue:** Did Huneau suffer an injury as a result of the negligence of the employees of Maple Ski Ridge?

**Rule:** To assert a negligence claim Huneau must have in fact suffered an injury.

**Analysis:** In this section show that Huneau could establish by a preponderance of the evidence that he suffered an injury.

**Conclusion:** A jury could [or could not] find that Huneau suffered an injury.

### 5. FIFTH ELEMENT OF HUNEAU'S THEORY OF THE CASE— DUTY

**Issue:** Did Maple Ski Ridge, Inc. owe a duty of care to Huneau?

**Rule:** A person who participates in athletic pursuits like snow tubing assumes the risk of injuries inherent in such pursuits. However, the operator of the athletic activity like a ski mountain has a duty of care not to increase the risks beyond those risks inherent in the activity of snow tubing.

**Analysis:** In this section show that Huneau could establish by a preponderance of the evidence that the Maple Ski Ridge employees increased the risks beyond those ordinarily undertaken in snow tubing and thereby had a duty of care to Huneau.

**Conclusion:** Huneau could [or could not] establish that Maple Ski Ridge owed a duty of care to Huneau.

The IRAC formula may be used even where a particular element of the theory of the case is not in dispute. The absence of a dispute over a particular element does not mean that the plaintiff escapes from the burden of establishing each element. The burden of proof remains always on the plaintiff to establish all of the elements necessary to sustain its cause of action.

Of the five elements in the *Huneau* case, the issues most likely to be litigated would be duty, negligence, and causation. If this were a case in a law office, however, the lawyer would want to analyze all five of the elements to make sure that the proof was sufficient to establish each element and that no element was overlooked. The IRAC analysis would be applied to the other elements of Huneau's cause of action not discussed in this example, such as the amount of damages to be awarded to Huneau as compensation for his injury, or the allocation of damages based on Huneau's comparative fault in causing his own injury. In answering an exam question the law student would most likely give more attention to the elements in dispute. The IRAC formula, regardless, provides the analytical structure to resolve each of the individual issues created by, or emerging from, the macro theory of the case.

Generally there are several possible theories of the case. Cory Huneau, for example, might have raised other theories to support his claim, assuming, however, that the supporting facts were available. For example, perhaps conditions on the day of the injury were too icy and Maple Ski Ridge should have declared the day unsafe for snow tubing, or perhaps Maple Ski Ridge had put untrained employees in charge of tubing safety, or perhaps the construction of the tuber's get-off area was too narrow and hence unsafe. Each of these macro theories would raise related micro legal issues. The student would want to develop other reasonably viable theories and use the IRAC formula to test the legal viability of these additional theories of the case.

**CASE 3. The boy who fell from the tree: A case example applying the IRAC formula to analyze a theory of the case.** In this case a 16-year-old boy climbed 25 feet up a pine tree and was injured when he touched a high-voltage electric wire that passed through the branches of the tree. The boy sued the landowner who had leased the property to the boy's host. The boy's theory of the case was that the landowner had a duty to warn her tenant, the host of the 16-year-old boy, about the danger of the electric wires, and the breach of that duty caused the boy's injury. The landowner argued that she had no legal duty to warn the tenant about the readily visible electric wires. The appellate court agreed with the landowner and ruled that there was no duty to warn. The theory of the case and IRAC elements are indicated by footnotes.

## HECTOR TAGLE, plaintiff, v. DONNA JAKOB, defendant.

737 N.Y.Supp.2d 331 (N.Y. 2001)

**The Court:** Defendant Donna Jakob owned property with a one-family house in the Town of Reading, Schuyler Country. The rear 10 feet of the backyard were subject to an easement that New York State Electric and Gas Co. acquired in 1945. The Electric Company maintains utility poles and uninsulated, overhead electric wires running approximately 25 feet above the ground. Two wires run through a single pine tree growing in the defendant's yard. In 1996, Jakob leased the property to a tenant but did not inform the tenant that electric wires passed through the tree. Shortly after taking possession of the property, the tenant invited plaintiff Tagle, then 16 years old, to a midday barbeque, during which Tagle climbed the tree to a height above the wires. Tagle touched a wire and fell approximately 25 feet to the ground, suffering burns and other injuries.

[Theory] Tagle sued Jakob, the owner.[1] Jakob moved for summary judgment. The trial court denied Jakob's motion, finding triable issues of fact. Jakob appealed.

[Issue] We turn to Tagle's argument as to Jakob's failure to warn the tenant of the danger presented by the wires.[2]

[Rule] We have long held that a landowner has no duty to warn of an open and obvious danger. By contrast, a latent hazard may give rise to a duty to protect entrants from that danger. While the issue of whether a hazard is latent or open and obvious is generally fact-specific and thus usually a jury question, a court may determine that a risk was open and obvious as a matter of law when the established facts compel that conclusion, and may do so on the basis of clear and undisputed evidence.[3]

[Analysis] The case before us presents that situation [of clear and undisputed evidence]. The photograph of the tree and wires taken from the backyard—stipulated by Tagle at argument to be an accurate

---

1. **Theory of the case**—The judge does not fully state the theory of the case but assumes that the reader will discern the theory from the facts and discussion. The theory of the case was that the defendant Jakob was negligent in failing to warn the tenant of a latent hazard, the electric wires, and it was this failure to warn that caused the injury to the plaintiff Tagle. [Ed.]

2. **I—The Issue**: Did the landowner Jakob have a duty to warn the tenant of the hazard of the electric wires passing through the pine tree? [Ed.]

3. **R—The Rule**: The R in this case is really a standard. The duty is triggered by a latent hazard, but not by a hazard that is open and obvious. Such a standard makes all the facts surrounding the hazard relevant. The plaintiff, to state a prima facie case on the element of duty, must offer evidence sufficient to support that the inference of the hazard was latent. [Ed.]

portrayal of the scene at the time of the accident—shows two electric wires running above the ground, entering the property, passing into the tree, leaving the tree, and then exiting the property. Any observer reasonably using his or her senses would see the wires and the tree through which the wires passed. It is unimaginable that an observer could see the wires entering and leaving the tree and not know that the wires passed through it. In short, there is nothing that Jakob knew or should have known that was not readily obvious to the tenant.[4]

[Conclusion] We conclude that, as a matter of law, Jakob had no reason to expect that the tenant would not observe the hazard or any conceivable risk associated with it. We therefore hold that Jakob had no duty to warn the tenant of that hazard.[5]

### ANALYSIS

The existence of a duty to warn a tenant of an unsafe condition is a legal question, but whether there was a legal duty depended in turn on whether the hazard was latent or not. As the court stated, whether the condition was latent or open and obvious is usually fact-specific and is thus a question for the jury. Here it was not a question for the jury. The court looked at the picture of the tree and, as if talking directly to the tenant and the plaintiff, said that if the wires entered the tree on one side and exited on the other side, what should Tagle and the tenant expect to find in the middle of the tree?

The outline of the opinion is plainly visible. The opinion begins with a statement of facts. The statement of facts is followed by the plaintiff's theory of the case which is indicated but not explicitly set out. Tagle's theory was that the landowner Jakob was negligent in failing to warn the tenant of the danger. Having selected that theory, a legal issue emerges.

> Issue: Did the landowner Jakob have a duty to warn her tenant of the danger of the electric wires? Rule: A landowner has a duty to warn a tenant of a latent danger but has no duty to warn of open and obvious danger. Analysis: Under the facts of this case, a jury could not find by a preponderance of the evidence that the presence of the electric wires was a latent danger. Conclusion: A jury could not find that the danger was latent; hence, the defendant Jakob had no duty to warn her tenant.

---

4. **A—The Analysis:** Here the judge applied the applicable standard to the facts of this case and ruled that, on these facts, a jury could not possibly find the hazard to be latent. [Ed.]

5. **C—Conclusion:** The judge resolved the issue by finding that the landowner Jakob had no duty to warn the tenant of the electric hazard. [Ed.]

The judge did not announce each of these elements, but they are readily apparent when the opinion is analyzed. The more obvious the pattern, the easier the opinion is to comprehend.

Opinions vary widely in the order of outline followed and in how complete or abbreviated they address each element. Routinely, judicial opinions omit a full statement of the theory of the case and address only the key or deciding issue or issues arising out of the unstated theory of the case. For example, in the *Tagle* case, the court addressed only a single key issue: whether there was a duty to warn. The court not only omitted a full statement of the theory of the case, but also omitted discussion of other issues such as causation, injury, or comparative fault. Discussion of these issues was unnecessary, because at the appellate level, there was only a single issue before the court. Jakob, the defendant, was the appellant and had raised only the issue of duty to warn.

This pattern of omission of essential elements works just fine for the appellate judges because it simplifies their opinions. It does not work so well for students and practicing lawyers attempting to understand the opinions. The law student taking a law school examination, and the practicing lawyer in considering litigation, would have worked through all of the issues in order to fully understand the strengths and weaknesses of the case.

A law school essay examination's validity lies in its similarity to actual legal work. An essay examination presents a set of facts and asks the student to state what causes of action might successfully be brought. A high-scoring exam will use both the theory of the case and IRAC. The theory of the case will set out the broad outline of the plaintiff's claim and permit the student to identify individual legal or factual issues. These issues, in turn, will then be addressed through the application of a micro outline based on the IRAC formula.

# CHAPTER 4

# Motion to Dismiss a Complaint
## Legal Limits on the Theory of the Case

For a theory of the case to be viable, it has to be within legal limits as set out by the law of torts. A plaintiff in a negligence case, for example, is entitled to compensation for his or her pain and suffering associated with a physical injury, but generally not for pain and suffering experienced over someone else's injury. That is the law. Although the pain and suffering might be unbearable, the law has drawn a line between the two situations.

The judge acts as gatekeeper on the legal limits of a theory of the case. A defendant challenges the theory of the case usually with a motion to dismiss the complaint. When a tort theory is legally deficient, the judge should throw the plaintiff's complaint out of court immediately, without a trial, and without review of any of the underlying facts.

## A. THE THEORY OF THE CASE MUST BE LEGALLY VIABLE

**CASE 4. The death of Coco the dog: The theory of the case must meet legal standards.** Coco, a beloved family dog, was crushed to death by a speeding car while Coco's owners, a husband and wife, were walking Coco and two other dogs on a quiet residential street. The wife herself narrowly escaped being hit by the careless, speeding driver.

Coco's owners, Robert Johnson and his wife, sued. The defendant driver moved to dismiss the Johnsons' complaint insofar as it demanded compensation for their emotional distress over witnessing the death of Coco. The judge empathized with

THE DEATH OF COCO THE DOG

the Johnsons' emotional distress but dismissed the complaint. The Johnsons appealed.

---

**ROBERT P. JOHNSON [AND HIS WIFE], plaintiffs, v. CECILLE F. DOUGLAS, defendant.**
723 N.Y.Supp.2d 627 (Sup. Ct. Nas. Co. 2001)

**The Court:** Plaintiffs, husband and wife, have commenced an action to recover for the death of the family dog. According to the allegations in the verified complaint, the Johnsons were walking their three dogs on the side of the street on a quiet residential road in Lake Success when the defendant Cecille Douglas allegedly drove her automobile at an excess rate of speed striking the Johnsons' dog, Coco. Plaintiff wife claims that she was walking Coco when she leaped out of the path of the speeding automobile, narrowly escaping serious injury. Coco was not so fortunate and was crushed by the automobile.

Defendant Douglas has moved to dismiss the Johnsons' causes of action to recover for their emotional distress due to the witnessing of the death of their dog.

There is no doubt that some pet owners have become so attached to their family pets that the animals are considered members of the family. This is particularly true of owners of domesticated dogs who have been repeatedly referred to as "Man's Best Friend" and a faithful companion. The court can empathize with the Johnsons' alleged horrific viewing of the death of the family dog, Coco, at the mercy of an automobile. It is not inconceivable that pet owners would seek some remuneration for the death of a faithful and loyal friend. However, the law is clear that pet owners cannot recover for emotional distress based upon an alleged negligent or malicious destruction of a dog, which is deemed to be personal property.

The extension of such thinking would permit recovery for mental distress caused by the malicious or negligent destruction of other personal property (i.e., a family heirloom or prized school ring). Although we live in a particularly litigious society, the court is not about to recognize a tortious cause of action to recover for emotional distress due to the death of a family pet. Such an expansion of the law would place an unnecessary burden on the ever-burgeoning caseloads of the court in resolving serious tort claims for injuries to individuals. Therefore, defendant Douglas's motion for dismissal of plaintiffs' second and third causes of action for emotional distress injuries is granted because both causes of action are insufficient as a matter of law.

### ANALYSIS

Coco's owners' theory of the case was that Cecille Douglas was negligent in that her careless driving had killed the dog Coco and thereby caused the plaintiffs two injuries: the death of Coco and, second, the owners' emotional distress. But the law of the state did not allow compensation for witnessing the death of a pet dog caused by the negligence of the defendant. The court gave two reasons for dismissing the emotional distress claim. One was legal: the law did not permit such a recovery. The second was to restate the policy behind the legal rule: if plaintiffs could recover for their emotional attachment to animals, objects, and other kinds of personal property, there would be no end to litigation. Coco's owners still have a claim for the value of the dog which, however, would be far less compensation than they sought for their emotional injuries.

This is an example of why it is so important initially to organize the facts into a theory. Once organized, the legal issues can be efficiently addressed. In Coco's case, a critical legal issue emerged related to the last element of the theory, the injury element. One type of injury was legally compensable and one was not. While both injuries were simultaneously caused by the driver's negligence, the separate injuries required a separate legal analysis and, unfortunately, produced separate results.

Note that the judge used the IRAC formula without actually saying so. The issue was whether the plaintiffs might recover compensation for an emotional injury caused when the defendant ran over and killed Coco the dog. The judge assumed the plaintiffs' allegations were true and only addressed the discrete legal issue of whether such facts would permit judicially ordered compensation. To analyze this legal issue, the judge invoked both a rule and a principle.

The rule, which had been set out and adopted in earlier court decisions, was that a plaintiff was not entitled compensation for emotional distress caused by an injury to personal property such as a dog. According to the rule, the only fact that mattered was that the plaintiff's distress was caused solely by witnessing the death of the dog.

The principle the judge invoked expanded the analysis beyond the facts of the case. Allowing compensation for a purely emotional injury would, the judge declared, open the door to a vast number of claims associated with injuries to all sorts of personal items like family heirlooms and school rings. This, the judge said, would tend to overwhelm the courts and distract limited judicial time away from dealing with more serious and irreplaceable losses. The conclusion, compelled in this case by both the rule and the principle, was that the owners of Coco could not recover despite the seriousness of their injuries. A contrary result could be argued, and the plaintiffs' lawyer no doubt made those arguments. The judge, however, got the last word.

**CASE 5. The infected wrestler: Unexpected facts may test the limits of tort law.** In this next case, the plaintiff, a high school wrestler, contracted herpes simplex from his opponent during a high school practice wrestling match. He sued his wrestling opponent, who was ill with the disease and who had failed to tell anyone. The complaint stated a novel theory of recovery, and the defendant moved to dismiss it. This time, the judge refused to dismiss the complaint.

**JOSEPH G. SILVER, plaintiff, v. LEVITTOWN UNION FREE SCHOOL DISTRICT AND DANIEL PATASCHER, defendants.**
692 N.Y.Supp.2d 886 (Sup. Ct. Nas. Cty 1999)

**The Court:** The complaint in this matter alleges that on November 30, 1996, Joseph Silver was a member of the Division Avenue High School wrestling team and was attending a team practice. Daniel Patascher, the defendant, was a former team member, having graduated in 1996, and was observing practice.

The complaint states that on the above date Patascher "suffered from the highly contagious 'herpes simplex' virus and bore wounds, blisters and/or rashes on and about his head and face." Silver was allegedly directed to wrestle Patascher and as a result came into direct contact with Patascher's "herpes simplex" virus, thereby contracting the disease.

The complaint asserts negligence by Patascher in "recklessly and/or intentionally failing to inform the plaintiff . . . that he suffered from the highly contagious 'herpes simplex' virus before engaging in the wrestling competition with the plaintiff."

Patascher now moves to dismiss the complaint for failure to state a cause of action. Patascher contends that there is no valid cause of action for the negligent transmission of a disease through casual contact, nor should there be. I agree with this premise but disagree that wrestling is "casual contact."

While the particular facts of this case present a novel issue of law, courts of this state have recognized a cause of action for both intentional and negligent transmission of sexually transmitted diseases.

As in any negligence action, the plaintiff must demonstrate that the defendant owed a duty of care to the plaintiff that was breached and proximately caused the condition alleged. A duty to disclose has been held to exist where the defendant knew or should have known that he or she had a communicable disease.

Contrary to Patascher's contention, the fact that the cited cases all involve instances of intimate sexual relations is not dispositive. It is the degree of contact, rather than its nature, sexual or otherwise, which creates the duty to disclose. Wrestling requires the participants to be in very close, intimate contact with each other. Therefore, the contact required in wrestling is far from casual contact. Due to the degree of contact involved in this sport, it is reasonable to impose a duty upon its participants to disclose the existence of serious communicable diseases. Although loathe to create new causes of action in tort, the law must nevertheless adapt to the society in which it exists.

Here the complaint sufficiently states a cause of action for negligent transmission of herpes simplex. Silver has alleged that Patascher knew of his condition and wrestled with Silver without disclosing the condition.

Accordingly, the motion to dismiss the complaint is denied, and the trial goes forward.

### ANALYSIS

The theory of the case advanced by Silver was that his injury was caused by Patascher's negligent failure to warn about his contagious disease. The challenge faced by Silver was that this theory had previously only been applied in cases where the transmission of the disease had occurred through sexual contact. Here the contact occurred during an athletic contest, wrestling.

The result reached in the opinion is paradigmatic of legal reasoning. In reviewing the law the judge found no rule or standard directly on point. Instead the judge discerned a principle that tied together prior cases and which could help to resolve the case before the court. The judge reasoned that what mattered in the prior cases where a duty to disclose had been found was the closeness of the contact. The fact that the contact in those prior cases had been of a sexual nature was only incidental.

Once having established that closeness of contact was the key principle underlying the prior decisions, the court could then answer the question of whether that principle applied in the wrestling context.

The issue was duty, a fundamental concept in tort law. To have a duty denotes that one person has a legally enforceable obligation to another. Every torts casebook and text emphatically explains that duty is an essential element in a tort case. There must be a duty of care running from the defendant to the plaintiff for the plaintiff to have a viable claim for damages. Duty is not, however, an element of the theory of the case. Why is that so? The answer is that duty is a legal conclusion, not a factual assertion or inference. Facts come first in the form of a theory of the case. Once the theory of the case organizes the facts, the judge can then consider the legal issue of duty.

In the infected wrestler's case, the critical facts were as follows: Patascher knew that he suffered from herpes simplex, a grave, serious disease that is spread by contact; he failed to disclose his illness to Silver; wrestling involves exceedingly close contact; and that close contact caused Silver's illness. These facts made up Silver's theory of the case.

The legal question arising out of this theory was whether Patascher had a duty to inform Silver of the illness. If he had a duty, his breach of the duty should result in liability. If he had no duty, his breach of failing to inform Silver would have no effect, and there would be no liability. This question of duty calls for a legal inquiry to be decided by the judge, not a factual inquiry to be decided by the jury. The judge was able to decide the legal question after the facts had been organized into a theory of the case.

Suppose instead that the defendant had given the plaintiff a nasty cold by coughing in plaintiff's presence without covering his mouth. Would these facts support a duty of care and, hence, liability? The theory of the case would be that the defendant was negligent in that he coughed without covering his mouth and that this negligent conduct caused the plaintiff to suffer the injury of a cold. The question for the court would be whether the coughing defendant had a duty of care to avoid spreading his cold by coughing without covering his mouth. The law does not recognize such a duty of care. Because there was no close intimate contact, the principle applied by the judge in the wrestling case would not apply to the coughing case. Coughing in public may be a breach of good manners and impolite, but having a cold and coughing in public does not trigger a legal duty of care recognized by the common law. The plaintiff loses on a legal point, not a factual one. The plaintiff developed a complete theory of the case but could not identify an underlying legal duty to support the theory. Even if the defendant gave the plaintiff a cold during the wrestling match, the plaintiff would still be out of luck. In that circumstance the difference between the seriousness of the disease and the ease of general transmission would likely block the finding of duty.

Duty is an essential condition for tort liability to attach, but duty is not an organizing fact. It is a legal conclusion that follows from factual allegations organized initially into the theory of the case. Duty, as a result, is not an element in the theory of the case.

Many difficult tort issues deal with the existence or nonexistence of duty. For example, tort law struggles over whether a person has a duty to rescue another person who is helpless and in danger. No matter how a duty issue presents itself, the place to begin the analysis is with organizing the facts into a theory of the case.

**CASE 6. The ex-wife secretly buried in the family plot: Legal limits include non-tort law rules.** The rules of civil procedure also set limits on torts cases. One such limit involves the timeliness of the plaintiff's complaint.

The next case involves family planning that went badly awry. When the family members arrived at the cemetery to bury their late son they found an interloper buried in the last spot in the family plot.

The family did not take this lying down. They demanded that the cemetery remove the interloper, whom they claimed was trespassing on their property. They alleged as an additional theory that the cemetery, by allowing the unauthorized burial, had negligently caused them severe emotional distress. The defendant cemetery defended against the claim of negligent infliction of emotional distress by arguing that the family brought its complaint too late.

THE EX-WIFE SECRETLY BURIED IN THE FAMILY PLOT

### RICHARD AUGERI ON BEHALF OF THE DECEASED SALVATRICE AUGERI, plaintiff, v. ROMAN CATHOLIC DIOCESE OF BROOKLYN AND ST. JOHN'S CEMETERY, defendants.
639 N.Y.Supp.2d 640 (4th Dep't 1996)

**The Court:** In 1918 Salvatrice Augeri purchased a lot containing six cemetery plots in defendant St. John's Cemetery, operated by defendant Roman Catholic Diocese of Brooklyn. From then until 1972, the remains of five Augeri family members were buried in the plots. Salvatrice's son, Domenick Augeri, died in 1989. Endeavoring to inter Domenick's remains in the sixth plot, the surviving members of the Augeri family learned from St. John's that the sixth plot was occupied by the body of Domenick's estranged wife, Anna Marra, who had abandoned Domenick after a short marriage in 1949. Following Anna Marra's death in 1984, Marra's son, Harry Taggart, who is unrelated to the Augeri family, represented to St. John's that he is the grandson and sole heir of the lot owner and that Anna Marra was Salvatrice's daughter. Relying on Taggart's representation, St. John's interred Anna Marra's remains in the sixth Augeri plot. Domenick's remains were then interred in another cemetery in a plot belonging to Domenick's sister, Salvatrice Augeri Mandarino.

The Augeri family asked St. John's to disinter Anna Marra's remains so that Domenick could be laid to rest in the family plot. St. John's refused to do so without a court order, and in 1991 the Augeri family commenced this action to compel St. John's to disinter Anna Marra's remains, and to transfer and inter Domenick's remains at St. John's expense, and for damages for the negligent infliction of emotional distress.

St. John's in 1992 moved to dismiss the Augeri family's complaint for failure to state a cause of action and on statute of limitations grounds. The trial court denied the motion and refused to dismiss the complaint as untimely.

We rule that the trial court properly denied St. John's motion insofar as it sought dismissal for failure to state a cause of action. With respect to the cause of action for negligent infliction of emotional distress, the Augeri families have stated grounds upon which relief can be granted. Because the alleged negligence of St. John's interfered with the proper disposal of Domenick's remains, damages may be recovered for resulting emotional harm. In addition, although not specifically alleged, the Augeri family has sufficiently stated the elements of a cause of action for trespass, consisting of the intentional entry by St. John's onto the Augeri family's land and the wrongful use without justification or consent.

With respect to the statute of limitations, while the underlying facts of the Augeri family's cause of action for negligent infliction of emotional distress occurred in 1984 when Marra was buried, the Augeri family did not sustain emotional harm until discovery of those facts in 1989. In their 1991 complaint, the Augeri family averred that they had no notice that the sixth plot was occupied and that there was no indication that it was occupied. The cause of action for negligent infliction of emotional distress did not accrue until all of the elements, including damages, could be truthfully alleged in the complaint. Because this action was commenced in 1991 within three years of discovery of the improper burial in 1989, it is not barred by the statute of limitations.

### ANALYSIS

St. John's Cemetery raised two legal arguments as to why the Augeri family's emotional distress claim should be dismissed: the theory of emotional distress was not legally viable, and, in any event, the complaint was filed too late. The judge ruled in favor of the Augeri family and against St. John's Cemetery on both grounds.

Under the common law, there is a duty to avoid the negligent handling of dead bodies. The breach of that duty is one of the areas where an injured plaintiff can recover for pure emotional distress. It is easy to understand why. In an event reported by the *New York Daily News* some years ago, for example, an airline lost the dead body of a woman it was transporting for burial from Israel to New York City. The son was quoted as saying that "Everyone knows how upsetting it is when an airline loses your luggage. Can you imagine how it feels when an airline loses your mother's body?"

The second legal reason raised by the court was that the complaint was filed too late. Every state has a statute of limitations that sets the time frame during which a complaint must be filed. If a plaintiff files too late, the claim is subject to dismissal. The limitation periods for various torts may be as short as one year or as long as six or more years after the injury. Time limitations are rules governed by state statute, and they vary by type of tort and from state to state.

In this case St. John's Cemetery argued that the time period started to run in 1984, the date of Anna Marra's secret burial, while the Augeri family argued that it began in 1989, when they discovered Anna Marra's body in the grave. The statute of limitations for the tort of negligent infliction of emotional distress was three years. If the court had measured the time period from 1984, the date of the burial, the Augeri family's claim would have been time-barred and the complaint dismissed. Instead the court ruled that the time period should be measured from the date of the Augeri's surprising discovery, and, as a result, the family's complaint slid in under the wire.

# CHAPTER 5

# The Prima Facie Case

## A. EVIDENCE MUST SUPPORT EVERY ELEMENT OF THE THEORY OF THE CASE

A plaintiff must not only have a theory of the case, a plaintiff must also produce sufficient evidence to establish a prima facie case. A prima facie case consists of provable facts that, taken together, support the plaintiff's theory of the case, and do so with sufficient persuasiveness that a jury could find the defendant liable.

Evidence means proof in the form of witnesses and documents; lawyers cannot make up proof. A theory without proof is like a building without a foundation. It will not stand up when tested.

The judge, acting as gatekeeper, asks this question: Has the plaintiff presented evidence in support of his or her theory of the case of sufficient persuasiveness that the jury could reasonably hold the defendant liable for the plaintiff's injury? The judge answers the question by applying a test of probability to the evidence: Could a jury find, more likely than not, that the plaintiff has proved his or her case? Not that the jury *must* find, only that it *could* find. If the answer is yes, the plaintiff has established a prima facie case and the trial proceeds to conclusion. If the plaintiff fails to establish a prima facie case, the judge ought to dismiss the plaintiff's complaint.

The judge does not make the ultimate decision in the case. That is for the jury. This is one of the basic differences between the judge and the jury.

The language used by judges in their opinions often blurs the concepts of theory of the case and prima facie case, but the concepts are quite distinct.

- A theory of the case presents the factual basis for why the defendant should compensate the plaintiff.
- A prima facie case demonstrates that the plaintiff can produce the minimum evidence necessary to prove his or her theory of the case.

## B. THE THEORY OF THE CASE MUST BE FACTUALLY VIABLE

**CASE 7. A puddle in the stairwell: A plaintiff with four theories and no supporting facts invites dismissal.** In this case a woman tripped while ascending a staircase in the defendant Housing Authority's building, injuring herself. The woman sued the Housing Authority for compensation and advanced four theories on why the Housing Authority should be liable and compensate her for her injury.

There was no dispute as to what happened in the stairwell. The plaintiff stepped over a puddle, which the judge decorously calls a liquid substance, and tripped. The plaintiff came up with four different theories. She did this either by adding additional facts to the basic, undisputed facts, or by suggesting new interpretations of facts that were not in dispute. In reading the court's opinion you should identify each of the plaintiff's four theories and note why the plaintiff in each instance failed to achieve a prima facie case.

**LAVERN JENKINS, plaintiff, v. NEW YORK CITY HOUSING AUTH., defendant.**
784 N.Y.Supp.2d 32 (1st Dep't 2004)

**The Court:** While ascending a staircase in the Housing Authority's building, plaintiff Lavern Jenkins attempted to bypass the third stair, which was covered on the right side by a puddle of some liquid substance, by stepping from the second stair directly to the fourth stair. Jenkins testified that she ascended on the right side of the staircase, holding the handrail on that side as she stepped over the puddle. However, Jenkins' left foot slipped as she placed it on the fourth stair, and she fell, fracturing her ankle. Jenkins subsequently commenced this personal injury action against the Housing Authority. For the reasons set forth below, we find that the Housing Authority's motion for summary judgment dismissing the complaint should have been granted.

To the extent Jenkins' claim is based on the Housing Authority's failure to remedy the transient hazardous condition allegedly created by the puddle on the third stair, Jenkins failed to offer any evidence rebutting the Housing Authority's showing that its staff had no actual or constructive notice of the presence of the puddle prior to the subject accident.

To the extent Jenkins relies on the theory that the accident was proximately caused by inadequate illumination, she admitted at her deposition that she could see the steps and the liquid substance before she fell, and, in opposing the summary judgment motion, she offered no evidence that her fall was precipitated by any hazard she failed to see due to poor lighting.

Similarly, Jenkins cannot prevail on her claim that the staircase, which had a handrail on the right side only, should have had handrails on both sides, because she failed to offer any evidence indicating that the omission of a left-side handrail (alongside the wall) was a proximate cause of her fall. On this record, it would be sheer speculation to conclude that, had there been a left-side handrail, Jenkins would have walked on the left side of the stairway to avoid the puddle, rather than walking on the right side and skipping a stair.

Finally, the opinion of Jenkins' expert does not raise a triable issue as to whether the surface of the stairs offered sufficient slip-resistance, because the expert did not identify the basis for the 0.5 coefficient-of-friction value he utilized as a standard. In this regard, we further note that Jenkins testified that she had never previously experienced any problems on the subject stairway, notwithstanding that she had used it several times per week for five years.

[The opinion ends with the court directing the trial court clerk to enter judgment in favor of the Housing Authority and to dismiss Jenkins' complaint for failing to state a cause of action.]

### ANALYSIS

Jenkins' four theories were that the Housing Authority was negligent in that

- It failed to clean up the puddle.
- It failed to provide adequate stairway lighting.
- It failed to provide a left-side handrail.
- It failed to provide slip-resistant stairs.

To deconstruct the opinion, the place to start is the theory of the case. Lavern Jenkins' theory was that Housing Authority employees were negligent in that they failed to address unsafe conditions in the stairs, and that their failure to address the unsafe conditions caused her injury. In analyzing that theory the judge followed an IRAC format. The Issue was whether Jenkins could produce a prima facie case that, for example, the absence of adequate lighting in the stairs caused her injury. The Rule in this instance is a standard. To establish her prima facie case concerning causation Jenkins had to produce sufficient evidence from which the jury could find that inadequate lighting was a substantial cause of her injury. In the Analysis part of the IRAC formula (the only part of the formula that is actually in the opinion), the judge reviewed the evidence and ruled that Jenkins had failed to produce a prima facie case of inadequate lighting because in her deposition she admitted that she saw both the steps and the liquid. The Conclusion was that Jenkins could not produce a prima facie case that inadequate lighting caused her injury.

Any of Jenkins' theories might have been adequate except that Jenkins lacked facts to support them. In litigation terms, Jenkins had theories, but no proof. Because of this failure to establish a prima facie case, the judge dismissed the complaint.

**CASE 8. The boy who fell from the roof: Possible explanations do not make a prima facie case.**  A boy fell from the roof of a Bronx apartment house and was killed. No one saw him fall. The theory of the case was that the owner of the building was negligent in that it allowed children to play on the roof knowing that the roof's parapet was too low to protect a child from falling, and it was the defective low parapet that caused the boy's death. The defendant challenged the assertion in the theory of the case that the low parapet caused the boy to fall.

---

**JOSE R. VELEZ, plaintiff, v. 1163 HOLDING LTD. AND YAUCO HOLDING CORP., defendants.**
626 N.Y.Supp.2d 795 (1st Dep't 1995)

**The Court:** This is a wrongful death action arising from the death, on May 18, 1991, of Jose R. Velez, the 11-year-old child, who allegedly fell to his death from the roof of an apartment building owned by defendant 1163 Holding Ltd. and located at 1161-1163 Stratford Avenue in the Bronx. According to the police report, the child's body was found face-down in the alleyway between the 1161-1163 building and a similar adjoining building owned by defendant Yauco Holding Corp.

Plaintiff Velez's theory of liability is premised on the claim that defendant 1163 Holding violated its common law duty to maintain its premises in a reasonably safe condition by permitting and allowing youngsters on the roof of their premises when the parapet wall was a mere 20 inches in height, thus creating a foreseeable risk that an individual on their roof would fall over by leaning too far over the wall, or tripping near the parapet.

Here, however, where there were no eyewitnesses to the child's fall, there was no evidence from which an inference of causation may be drawn. It was just as likely that the child's fall from the roof had nothing to do with the parapet as that it did.

Therefore, under the circumstances herein, any finding of proximate cause would be impermissibly speculative and, even after viewing the evidence in the light most favorable to the plaintiff, there is no showing that the alleged defect was the proximate cause of the decedent's fall.

The complaint against the defendant 1163 Holding Ltd. is dismissed.

### ANALYSIS

The plaintiff's theory of the case hinged on the illegality of the parapet. Because the parapet was substandard, why shouldn't the building owner be made to pay something anyway?

We know two things for sure: the parapet was low and the boy died when he fell from the roof. Despite these facts, the court treated the claim for compensation as entirely speculative and refused to send the case to the jury. How could the judge call the boy's theory speculative?

One way to answer that question is to list all the plausible scenarios for the fall. The boy might have tripped and fallen over the low parapet. But he also might have slipped while standing on the parapet as a dare or for the fun of it. He might have committed suicide by jumping. Now ask whether the height of the parapet increased or decreased the risk of these various scenarios. Are there any facts from which one could logically infer the cause of the fall?

The standard by which judges evaluate a plaintiff's evidence is whether a jury could rationally conclude that the theory of the case is, more likely than not, the correct scenario. If a jury could rationally so conclude, then the judge should submit the case to the jury. But if a jury could not rationally reach that conclusion, then the judge would be justified in describing the theory of the case by the epithet of speculation.

In the boy's case, the judge ruled that the jury could not rationally conclude that it was more likely than not that the parapet caused the fall. It was equally possible that the boy committed suicide or climbed the parapet in a dare. It was the equality of the possibilities that doomed the boy's claim. In the judge's view there was no rational way to explain why one possibility was more likely than the other.

## C. WHAT A PERSON KNOWS MUST BE INFERRED FROM OTHER FACTS

Many tort theories depend on proof of the mental state of the plaintiff or defendant. What a person knew or should have known is always proved indirectly by inference from other facts.

**CASE 9. The dog that bit the bartender: When specific knowledge is part of a prima facie case, knowledge must be inferred from other facts.** The plaintiff in this case invoked one of the most ancient common law tort theories: an owner of a dog or other domesticated animal is held strictly liable for any injury the animal causes if the owner had prior knowledge of the animal's vicious nature. To be strictly liable means that the owner is liable regardless of fault. All the victim has to prove is that the owner had prior knowledge of the animal's vicious propensities. The victim would not also have to prove, for example, that the owner was negligent in handling or restraining the animal.

The facts of this case read like a TV beer commercial. A large, normally docile Akita named Diesel, who was given free range to wander about a tavern, observed a fight between two human patrons, and, subsequently, without apparent provocation, bit the off-duty female bartender who was petting it on the flanks. The bit bartender sued Diesel's owner and the owner of the bar.

---

### KYLA MCKEE, plaintiff, v. J&J OTSEGO PROPERTIES INC., D/B/A COACH'S CORNER, AND JOSEPH VAN ORDEN, defendants.
716 N.Y.Supp.2d 739 (3rd Dep't 2000)

**The Court:** Kyla McKee was bitten by a dog owned by defendant Joseph Van Orden on premises known as Coach's Corner, a tavern owned by J&J Otsego Properties Inc. in the City of Oneonta, Otsego County. According to McKee, who worked as a bartender at the tavern but who had completed her shift and was off duty at the time of the incident, Van Orden arrived at the bar shortly before 6:00 P.M. on November 20, 1997, accompanied by his dog, "Diesel," a 90-pound Akita. Because Coach's Corner had a policy of prohibiting dogs on the premises, McKee asked Fred Morris, the manager of the bar, to speak to Van Orden about removing the dog. However, sometime later, Morris apparently indicated that the dog could remain. Having been released from his leash, the dog moved freely within the bar without disturbing the approximately eight customers who were in the establishment.

After a loud argument erupted between two patrons, Morris expelled the troublesome customers from the tavern. Although the dog paced nervously during the dispute, he calmed down after the commotion ended. Fifteen to twenty minutes later, McKee asked Van Order for permission to pet Diesel, who was then sitting quietly next to him, and Van Orden assented. McKee squatted next to the dog with her face inches from the animal's face and began to pet its flanks, initially eliciting no response from the dog. However, moments later, Diesel, suddenly turned his head and bit McKee in the face, causing lacerations. Van Orden, who was within three feet of the dog, immediately pulled the animal away from McKee and removed him from the bar.

McKee commenced this personal injury action against Van Orden and J&J Otsego Properties, alleging that they knew or should have known of the animal's vicious propensities and were negligent in allowing the dog to be unrestrained on the premises. After the parties engaged in discovery, both Van Orden and J&J Properties moved for summary judgment, asserting McKee failed to establish a basis for liability as there was no indication the dog had vicious propensities. McKee opposed the motions, arguing there was evidence of vicious propensities. The trial court dismissed the complaint, finding that McKee failed to offer any evidence that Diesel possessed vicious propensities.

Generally, a plaintiff may not recover in strict liability for injuries sustained in an attack by a dog without establishing that the animal had vicious propensities and that the defendant knew or should have known of such propensities. Upon our review of the record, we concur with the trial court's finding that no evidence was presented from which it could be inferred that Diesel possessed vicious propensities, or that Van Orden or J&J Properties could or should have been aware of such propensities. Van Orden's assertion that the dog had never bitten anyone before and was generally friendly with strangers was not contradicted, and by all accounts, the dog was not aggressive and did not behave in a threatening manner while in the bar prior to the incident.

[The court affirmed the trial court's decision to dismiss McKee's complaint.]

### ANALYSIS

Here the defendants testified that Diesel was docile as a kitten, and that they had no reason to suspect that Diesel possessed a vicious propensity. McKee apparently could find no prior victims of Diesel or other incidents from which it could be inferred that the owner did in fact have knowledge of the dog's vicious propensity. This left plaintiff McKee with no evidence except a narration of the events in the tavern, and that narration, the judge ruled, was insufficient to establish the requisite knowledge on behalf of Diesel's owners.

# CHAPTER 6

# Summary Judgment and Fact Issues

## A. MOTION FOR SUMMARY JUDGMENT CHALLENGES THE SUFFICIENCY OF THE PLAINTIFF'S PRIMA FACIE CASE

A defendant's motion for summary judgment is a moment of truth for the plaintiff, who must lay out proof in sufficient detail to support his or her theory of the case in order to avoid dismissal. It is equally critical for the defendant, who, by the motion, mounts the most persuasive case possible in an attempt to avoid a trial and liability.

Most often it is the defendant who makes a motion for summary judgment, but either party may make the motion. When the defendant moves for summary judgment, the defendant is asking the trial judge to dismiss the plaintiff's complaint. When a plaintiff moves for summary judgment, the plaintiff asks the judge to grant the plaintiff a judgment without a trial.

The parties usually submit affidavits, documents, transcripts of depositions, and other relevant evidence in support of, or in opposition to, a motion for summary judgment. Submission of evidence by the parties distinguishes a motion for summary judgment from a motion to dismiss a complaint. A motion to dismiss the complaint is addressed solely to the theories contained in the complaint, while a motion for summary judgment takes into account facts and evidence beyond those facts and tests whether the plaintiff can offer sufficient proof in support of the complaint.

Judges in their opinions often conflate the two motions by describing a defendant's motion for summary judgment as a "motion for summary judgment to dismiss the complaint." The difference between the motions is this:

- A motion to dismiss a complaint tests the **legal** sufficiency of the plaintiff's theory of the case.

- A motion for summary judgment tests the **factual** sufficiency of the plaintiff's prima facie case.

If there are no triable fact issues on which reasonable people could differ, the judge should grant summary judgment. If one or more disputes concerning a material fact can reasonably be debated, the judge should deny the motion and continue to trial.

The most obvious kind of triable issue occurs when there is a dispute about what happened. For example, two cars collide at an intersection with a traffic signal. Was the traffic signal red, green, or yellow when the plaintiff's car entered the intersection? The plaintiff testifies that it was green and that he had the right-of-way. The defendant counters with testimony that the signal was red and therefore the plaintiff did not have the right-of-way. The dispute between the parties about the color of the signal, a material fact in this case, presents a triable issue.

There is a second major kind of triable issue in a negligence case. This is the question of negligence itself. Such a finding is both factual and judgmental: not only did the defendant do it, but that conduct fell below a reasonable standard of care. The jury's finding describes the conduct factually (the defendant ran the red light), and characterizes that conduct as negligent when measured against a standard of care: a driver using reasonable care would not have run the red light in these circumstances. Both factual findings are essential to a legal conclusion settling the rights as between the parties.

More than one triable issue may arise out of a single event: for example, did the driver drive through a red light (fact issue one); was the driver's conduct in driving through the red light negligent or was it excused for some reason like being chased through by an ambulance with its siren wailing (fact issue two); if the driver's conduct were negligent, did that negligence cause the plaintiff's injury (fact issue three); and how much compensation should the defendant pay for having caused the injury (fact issue four). All four fact issues would be decided by the jury.

The jury, in resolving triable fact issues, uses the preponderance of the evidence standard: it must decide which of the possibilities is more likely than not.

It is very important to separate out the individual fact issues and analyze each one separately. If the lawyer lumps fact issues together, there will be no clarity. But separate fact issues and you will begin to think like a lawyer.

**Here is the importance of establishing a triable fact issue: If there is a triable fact issue, the case stays in court and must go to the jury for resolution.** Staying in court and not being dismissed is the paramount strategic goal of the plaintiff's attorney.

## B. WHEN A MATERIAL FACT OR INFERENCE IS IN DISPUTE, THE RESULT IS A TRIABLE FACT ISSUE TO BE DECIDED BY THE JURY

**CASE 10.  The woman who tripped on her own rope: Opposing inferences may create a triable fact issue.** In this case a short, elderly woman tripped on a dangling rope that she herself had tied to a garage door handle. She needed the rope to close the garage door that, because it was broken, would remain open only in the fully raised position. When fully raised, the elderly woman was too short to reach the door, so she closed the garage door by pulling on the dangling rope.

The plaintiff's theory of the case was that the landlord was negligent in not repairing the garage door that caused the short, elderly woman to tie the rope, trip on the rope, and injure herself.

The defendant landlord's counter theory of the case was that the elderly woman caused her own injury because she tied the rope on which she tripped and therefore she must have known of its presence.

---

**JEAN SPATHOS, plaintiff, v. GRAMATAN MANAGEMENT, INC., defendant.**
770 N.Y.Supp.2d 130 (2d Dep't 2003)

**The Court:** The plaintiff Jean Spathos was injured when she caught her foot in a rope and fell in an attached garage in the housing complex where she resided. The complex was managed by the defendant Gramatan Management. According to the plaintiff Spathos, the garage door was defective because it was only secure when opened to its fullest extent, and she had tied a rope to the handle of the garage door to allow her to close it from that height. The defendant Gramatan Management admitted it had been aware of the defective condition of the door for two or three years but failed to correct it. During this period it was also aware that the plaintiff Spathos was using the rope in order to close the door. Gramatan Management moved for summary judgment, contending that the attachment of the rope by plaintiff Spathos was a superseding, intervening cause of her injury. The trial court granted Gramatan Management's motion for summary judgment. We reverse.

It is well settled that a plaintiff's action that is extraordinary and unforeseeable will be deemed a superseding cause that severs the causal connection between the defendant's negligence and the plaintiff's injuries.[6] Whether a plaintiff's act is a superseding cause or whether it is a normal consequence of the situation created by a defendant are typically questions to be determined by the trier of fact.

The defendant Gramatan Management failed to establish as a matter of law that the plaintiff's actions were a superseding cause absolving it from liability. Triable issues of fact exist as to whether it was foreseeable that the plaintiff Spathos would attempt to overcome the defective condition of the garage door that the defendant had neglected to correct for such a prolonged period of time.

[The case was sent back to the trial court for trial.]

### ANALYSIS

There was no dispute between the parties over what happened, only the inferences to be drawn from the facts. Spathos urged in opposition to the motion for summary judgment that a jury could find that Gramatan Management's conduct was negligent in that it allowed a defective door to remain in use with the predictable consequences that someone would get hurt. Gramatan Management in support of its motion urged that the danger, if there was any, was fully known by Spathos and she has only herself to blame.

Spathos of course had tied the rope herself, had regularly used it to open and close the garage, and then tripped on her own handiwork. The unusual fact that Spathos had both tied the rope and regularly used it allowed Gramatan Management to argue that she was the sole cause of her own injury, and it is that issue that the court ruled must go to the jury: Whether or not Gramatan Management proximately caused Spatho's injury was a triable issue that had to be decided by the jury.

---

6. All the judge is saying here is that the defendant is not liable to the plaintiff if the plaintiff's own actions caused her own injury. The defendant may have done something negligent like not fixing the garage door, but liability based on that negligence dissipates in light of the plaintiff's own negligent act of tripping on her own rope. [Ed.]

**CASE 11. The icy stairs at the school: Credibility of witnesses may create a triable fact issue.** In this case a school bus monitor on a mission of mercy slipped on an allegedly icy staircase. The custodial crew of the defendant Gloversville Enlarged School District regularly removed ice and had no knowledge of the alleged icy condition. The injured school bus monitor was able to establish her prima facie case by producing testimony tending to show that the condition had existed for a sufficient length of time for the school district to notice the ice and remove it.

**ELAINE M. UHLINGER, plaintiff, v. GLOVERSVILLE ENLARGED SCHOOL DISTRICT, defendant.**
796 N.Y.Supp.2d 437 (3rd Dep't 2005)

**The Court:** Plaintiff Elaine M. Uhlinger, a bus monitor, was injured when she fell on the steps outside one of Gloversville's schools as she was delivering a student's medication to the school nurse. Defendant Gloversville moved for summary judgment dismissing Uhlinger's complaint. The trial court granted Gloversville's motion based on the lack of notice of any dangerous condition.

Liability for a slip and fall may not be imposed upon a landowner unless there is evidence that the landowner knew or, in the exercise of reasonable care, should have known that icy conditions existed, yet failed to correct the situation. This is the constructive notice standard (i.e., that the condition "was visible and apparent and existed for a sufficient period of time prior to the accident to permit defendant to discover it and take corrective action").

There was no actual notice here. To prove a lack of constructive notice, Gloversville offered proof from its custodial crew regarding its regular procedure of snow removal and spreading a salt/sand mixture each winter day on all steps and walkways before students and staff arrive. Gloversville does not keep records of the weather conditions or its snow or ice removal actions. None of the custodial crew could specifically remember any such actions taken on the day of Uhlinger's fall.

To create questions of fact, Uhlinger submitted affidavits of a bus driver who observed packed ice and snow on the top step and the walkway leading to the steps on which Uhlinger fell, with no evidence of salt or sand on those areas. Another witness affirmed that the steps were "coated with ice," again with no evidence of any melting agent. While the freeze/thaw theory expounded by plaintiff Uhlinger's expert meteorologist was speculative, his meteorological data pointed out that approximately five inches of snow fell over the day or two before Uhlinger's fall and no precipitation fell for approximately eight hours prior to her fall.

We find these submissions sufficient to create questions of fact regarding notice of the icy conditions and ample time to take corrective action.

[The court sent the case back to the trial court to resolve the factual dispute.]

### ANALYSIS

Gloversville's defense was that its custodians regularly cleared the snow and ice. The custodians, however, could not remember anything about the day of the event and kept no records of their efforts at snow removal.

To rebut Gloverville's evidence of a regular practice of snow and ice removal, the plaintiff produced affidavits from witnesses who allegedly saw the ice. This case presents a typical situation where the credibility of witnesses must be considered. Uhlinger submitted her facts through affidavits, which are written statements prepared, at a minimum, with the lawyer's assistance, and, more often, with the lawyer doing all of the writing and the witness only correcting and signing the affidavit. Testimony contained in the affidavit is still open to question and cross examination.

For example, one of Uhlinger's witnesses affirmed in her affidavit that the stairs were "coated with ice." Maybe. But how close was she to the staircase when she observed it? How good was her eyesight? When did she observe the staircase, before or after the accident? What does she mean by the term "coated with ice", anyway? If the staircase had been coated with ice, did the plaintiff actually slip on that part of the staircase or on some other part that may not have been coated with ice? And if the witness could see the ice, should not the plaintiff have also seen it? And when she observed the staircase, did she observe the custodians, and, if so, what were they doing?

These are the sorts of questions that the jury resolves. And that is why the case was sent back for trial.

**CASE 12. The cheerleader's dangerous stunt: Contrary narratives may create a triable fact issue.** A cheerleader performing a dangerous stunt was injured. She sued the school district. Her theory of the case was that the school district was negligent in that it did not properly supervise such dangerous activities. The cheerleader's coach testified, however, that she had prohibited the stunt, and, in any event, the cheerleader, by joining the team, accepted the risks normally a part of cheerleading. This was a fairly strong position, yet the cheerleader defeated the school district's motion for summary judgment by putting into issue every one of the school district's factual assertions.

---

**CHANTELLE DRIEVER, plaintiff, v. SPACKENKILL UNION FREE SCHOOL DISTRICT, defendant.**
798 N.Y.Supp.2d 145 (2d Dep't 2005)

**The Court:** A school district remains under a duty to exercise ordinary reasonable care to protect student athletes involved in extracurricular sports from unreasonably increased risks. While the infant plaintiff Chantelle Driever voluntarily participated in cheerleading activities and therefore assumed the risks to which her role exposed her, she did not assume those risks that were "unreasonably increased."

The defendant school district made a prima facie showing of entitlement to judgment as a matter of law by establishing that it provided adequate supervision, including, inter alia,[7] the coach's deposition testimony that she had prohibited the cheerleaders' stunt in question and that, in any event, the level of supervision was not a proximate cause of the plaintiff Driever's accident.[8]

In opposition, however, plaintiff Driever proffered sufficient evidence to raise a triable issue of fact as to whether plaintiff Driever's coach had prohibited the stunt, whether she was aware that the stunt would be performed notwithstanding dangerous wind conditions, and whether she failed to provide proper supervision of the cheerleading activities, thereby exposing plaintiff Driever to an unreasonably increased risk of injury. Therefore the trial court properly denied the school district's motion for summary judgment.

[The court sent the case back to the trial court for trial to resolve the fact issues and to decide the cause of the cheerleader's injury.]

---

### ANALYSIS

The court states that the plaintiff Driever "proffered sufficient evidence" to raise a triable issue with respect to the school district's supervision. The use of the word "proffer" in this sentence has a specific legal meaning. "Proffer"

---

7. Inter alia is a Latin phrase for "among other things." [Ed.]

8. This paragraph is a compressed restatement of the facts the school district relied upon to establish its prima facie entitlement to summary judgment. The evidence would have been far richer in facts, describing with particularity how the coaches supervised cheerleading practices and performances, and detailing the coach's prohibition of the trick in question. Based on this evidence, the court ruled that the school district established a prima facie entitlement to summary judgment, which compelled the cheerleader to respond with contrary facts sufficient to require a trial. [Ed.]

generally means to offer or suggest, but when used with respect to evidence, it generally means that the lawyer has informed the judge and the other side what a witness would testify if called to testify. In this case the proffer was most likely made by submitting a sworn statement by the plaintiff and perhaps other cheerleaders denying that the coach had prohibited the stunt or challenging the claim that the school district provided adequate supervision by reciting contrary facts.

The jury at trial will have to choose which narrative is more likely than not. The burden of persuasion is on the plaintiff. If the jury does not accept the cheerleader's narrative, she will lose her claim. The decision at trial will therefore turn on credibility. Did the coach really prohibit the stunt? Did she know that the stunt was to be performed anyway despite her prohibition? Credibility is generally an issue for the jury.

**CASE 13. If a man fell on ice, did the man slip on the ice? Circumstantial evidence may create a triable issue.** In the next case, a man was found dead and alone in his apartment. No one saw him get injured, and the decedent wrote nothing before he died. The wife and son of the decedent traced the dead man's steps along a trail of blood from his apartment back to a puddle of blood on an icy patch located on a sidewalk owned by the apartment house. They reasoned that the victim must have been injured when he slipped on the ice but was able to return to his apartment before he died of his injury.

The son, on behalf of the dead man, sued the apartment housing corporation on the theory that the corporation was negligent in that it failed to keep the sidewalk in a reasonably safe condition. The trial court declared the wife and son's testimony sufficient for a prima facie case, and the apartment housing corporation appealed.

**ALEXANDER LERNER, plaintiff, v. LUNA PARK HOUSING CORP., defendant.**
797 N.Y.Supp.2d 126 (2d Dep't 2005)

**The Court:** The plaintiff, the son of the deceased victim, succeeded in rebutting the defendant Luna Park's prima facie showing of entitlement to summary judgment as a matter of law. While there were no witnesses to the decedent's fall, deposition testimony from the decedent's wife and son regarding, inter alia, the trail of blood commencing in a puddle on a patch of ice and leading down a hallway to the decedent's apartment, provided sufficient circumstantial evidence to raise a triable issue of fact as to whether the decedent's fall was proximately caused by a patch of ice that the employees of Luna Park allegedly negligently failed to remove.

Moreover, the evidence offered by the plaintiff raised a triable issue of fact as to whether the subject patch of ice existed before commencement of a snowstorm[9] and therefore whether the employees of Luna Park could be charged with constructive notice of the dangerous condition. [The court affirmed the trial court.]

### ANALYSIS

The son had only circumstantial evidence to support his theory that the fall on the ice caused the father's death. Circumstantial evidence is defined as indirect evidence. Evidence may be direct or indirect depending on the inference asked to be drawn from the evidence.

If, for example, a witness testified that he personally saw the man slip and fall on the ice, the witness would be giving direct evidence because he could testify about what he personally saw. The son, however, testified only to seeing the trail and puddle of blood. His testimony was direct, but only with respect to what he saw, the trail of blood and puddle at the icy spot. His testimony was indirect and therefore only circumstantial with respect to whether the ice caused the man's fall. It is possible that the man got dizzy and fell by himself. There is a difference between a man falling on the ice and the ice causing the man's fall. The jury will have to decide whether the son's theory is supported by a preponderance of the evidence.

**CASE 14. The golf cart that ran over the golfer. Expert testimony cannot save an otherwise inadequate prima facie case.** In this next case, a golfer was run over by her own golf cart. The golfer sued the golf club's professional, Stephen Jennings, from whom the golfer had rented the golf cart. Her theory was that Jennings had not properly maintained the golf cart's brakes. Jennings proved that maintenance of the brakes had nothing to do with the injury.

THE GOLF CART THAT RAN OVER A GOLFER

---

9. The rule on snow and ice in New York State where this event occurred is that so long as the snow is falling, the owner does not have a duty to remove it. But once a reasonable time has passed after the snow has stopped falling, the owner has a duty to remove snow and ice and otherwise make the property reasonably safe. The existence of this rule explains why the son brought a weatherman into court who could testify that while snow fell that day, it did not begin until after the man had fallen. [Ed.]

## MARGUERITE R. BRUST, plaintiff, v. TOWN OF CAROGA, defendant.

731 N.Y.Supp.2d 542 (3rd Dep't 2001)

**The Court:** In 1996, plaintiff Marguerite Brust, an experienced golfer, played golf at the Nick Stoner Municipal Golf Course. As Brust had done on numerous other courses, she rented a golf cart, this time from defendant Stephen Jennings, who was employed by the Town of Caroga as its golf professional at the course.

After teeing off at the second hole, Brust drove her cart on the path and stopped perpendicular to the crest of a small hill in front of the green despite a sign labeled 'carts' with an arrow pointing parallel to the crest. After she removed a club and began to walk toward her ball, the cart rolled down the slope of the fairway, ultimately striking her and causing her injury. Burst testified that while her habit was to set the brake when stopping her cart, she could not recall if she did so on this occasion; she made this disclosure not only to the investigating police officer but also to the numerous other witnesses who assisted her at the scene. Jennings testified that minutes after the accident, he tested the braking mechanism of the golf cart and found it to be in proper working condition. This fact was confirmed by the testing of the cart at the accident scene by both a volunteer firefighter and a golfer in the group immediately behind plaintiff.

Brust commenced this negligence action against Jennings. Jennings moved for summary judgment, which the trial court granted.

The defendant Jennings, as the movant on the motion for summary judgment, bore the initial burden of tendering evidentiary proof in admissible form sufficient to demonstrate that judgment should be granted to him as a matter of law. Jennings met this prima facie burden by his tender of testimony from witnesses who detailed that upon their testing of the brakes on the cart immediately after the injury, they were shown to be in good working order. This tender was coupled with his own testimony concerning the implementation of his daily practice of checking the brakes both prior to and subsequent to all rentals.

The burden then shifted to Brust to produce evidentiary proof in admissible form sufficient to require a trial of material questions of fact. Brust's submission of an expert's report that concluded that the braking system was unsafe and inadequate, founded solely upon his review of Jennings' maintenance logs, was insufficient. Brust's own testimony did little to advance a triable issue of fact because she failed to establish that she had engaged the braking system on the cart immediately prior to her injury. For these reasons the trial court properly dismissed the action against Jennings.

## ANALYSIS

The fact issue in question was whether the defendant's negligence in maintaining the golf cart's brakes caused the plaintiff's injury. The plaintiff's expert based his testimony on a review of the maintenance logs and found that maintenance of the golf carts was not up to snuff. His testimony was relevant to identifying what the defendant may have done that was negligent. But the brakes, even if badly maintained, worked both before and after the accident. The golfer lacked proof linking the poor maintenance to a brake failure. Without that proof, the plaintiff failed to establish a triable fact issue, and Jennings was entitled to summary judgment.

**CASE 15. The woman who ate a worm: A leap of faith is not evidence.** In this case, a woman alleged that she became nauseous after seeing and possibly eating a worm that, she said, was negligently included in the contents of a can of A&P string beans. A&P argued that the woman failed to prove that its negligent conduct caused the nausea, and moved for summary judgment. The court agreed, and granted the motion.

THE WOMAN WHO ATE A WORM

---

**MARGARET VALENTI, plaintiff, v. GREAT ATLANTIC & PACIFIC TEA CO., defendant.**
615 N.Y.Supp.2d 84 (2nd Dep't 1994)

**The Court:** The plaintiff Margaret Valenti suffered nausea, vomiting, and diarrhea when she allegedly saw and/or ate a worm in a can of string beans that she purchased at a supermarket. Valenti, the plaintiff, had the burden of proving that the food was defective and that injury resulted from its consumption.

Valenti failed to submit any probative evidence that would establish that her flu-like symptoms were caused by the foreign object in the can of beans. The mere fact that Valenti became nauseous about one-half hour after consuming some of the contents of the can is insufficient to withstand A&P's motion for summary judgment. There are many different causes of nausea, vomiting, and stomach distress. Moreover, the report of Valenti's own physician, in describing her visit to his office the day after the alleged incident, makes no reference to the incident or to any examination or medication given in reference thereto. Valenti's evidence of impurity leaves her proof in the realm of speculation and conjecture.

[The court granted A&P's motion for summary judgment and dismissed Valenti's complaint.]

### ANALYSIS

Probative evidence is evidence that has the effect of proving or helping to prove the fact sought. The dispute in this case was whether the worm in the can caused the subsequent illnesses. Margaret Valenti's testimony describing how sick she became was probative for establishing her injury (her nausea and emotional distress) and for establishing the timing of the injury (i.e., shortly after eating the worm), but the testimony was not sufficiently probative on whether eating the worm actually caused the illnesses she experienced. Valenti, the court ruled, failed to establish a triable fact issue on causation.

This is a problem of logic. It is possible that Valenti's illnesses, which followed shortly after she saw and ate the worm, were caused by that event, but that conclusion is only a possibility. As the judge wrote, lots of other things could have caused the illnesses she experienced. To leap to the conclusion that the worm caused the illnesses is an example of the *post hoc, ergo propter hoc* error, Latin for "after it, therefore, due it." Just because one thing follows another in time does not prove that the first caused the second. For example, farmers suffering from drought might gather together and do a rain dance. It then rains. Did the rain dance cause the rain?

**CASE 16. The drunk but innocent driver: A defendant's opposing evidence may destroy the plaintiff's prima facie case entirely.** This next case involved a car accident. The mother, on behalf of the estate of her son who died in the accident, sued the driver of the other car who was legally drunk at the time of the accident. That should have been enough to make the drunk driver liable for the death. But the court ruled otherwise. The drunk driver showed that his drunkenness did not cause the accident.

## ELIZABETH WALLACE, plaintiff, v. FRANCIS D. TERRELL, defendant.

744 N.Y.Supp.2d 551 (3rd Dep't 2002)

**The Court:** Plaintiff Elizabeth Wallace is the executor of the estate of her son, Brent Wallace, who died as a result of injuries sustained in a March 1997 motor vehicle accident on State Route 81 in the Town of Coxsackie, Greene County. Wallace, driving at night in a heavy snowstorm, lost control of his vehicle on a downhill curve and skidded into the oncoming lane, where he was struck by defendant Terrell's vehicle. Although a court-ordered blood test showed Terrell's blood alcohol content to be 0.10 percent, establishing that he was legally intoxicated, the investigating authorities determined that his intoxication played no role in the accident.

Although Terrell's driving while intoxicated unquestionably constitutes negligence per se,[10] in order for liability to attach, it must also be proved that the negligence was the cause of the event that produced the harm. Therefore, Terrell's legal intoxication, without a showing of causation, cannot provide a basis for liability.

Terrell asserted that the Wallace vehicle unexpectedly skidded into his lane and that he braked but could not avoid the collision. Deposition testimony from both the state trooper who initially investigated the accident and the state police accident reconstruction expert concluded that there was no contributory fault on the part of Terrell. Terrell thus prima facie established that there was nothing he could have done to avoid the collision, and it was incumbent upon the lawyer for Wallace to submit evidence in admissible form to create an issue of fact as to Terrell's negligence contributing to the happening of the accident.

Specifically, the lawyer for Wallace needed to raise a question of fact as to whether the accident was more likely caused by Terrell's negligence than by some other factor.

The lawyer for Wallace contends that Terrell's intoxication would have slowed his reaction time and therefore contributed to the accident. However, the lawyer for Wallace offers no proof to establish that Terrell could have taken any kind of evasive action under the circumstances. As unsupported speculation is not sufficient to defeat a motion for summary judgment, we conclude that [the trial court] properly granted Terrell's motion.

---

10. 'Negligence per se' is a legal idiom meaning that the conduct was negligent as a matter of law. The term usually refers to conduct in violation of a statute such as the statute in this case that made driving while intoxicated a crime. The court's opinion distinguished between characterizing conduct as negligent and wrongful, which driving while drunk clearly was, and the separate element of a prima facie case that the negligent conduct in fact *caused* the injury. Causation is a fact issue. [Ed.]

### ANALYSIS

The plaintiff's theory of the case was that the drunk driver's slowed reaction time was a cause of the accident. To establish a triable fact issue on causation, the plaintiff argued that the drunk driver would have been able to avoid hitting the plaintiff's oncoming car had he not been drunk. But that theory was demolished by the accident report and the investigations by the state police that there was nothing that the drunk driver could have done once the plaintiff slid into the drunk driver's lane. A little equivocation on the police's part, and the plaintiff would have had a triable issue on causation for the jury. With police and accident investigation testimony so unequivocal, the jury could not rationally have concluded that the drunk driver was a cause of the accident, which is why, in the end, the court calls the plaintiff's argument an "unsupported speculation."

## C. WHEN A PLAINTIFF MOVES FOR SUMMARY JUDGMENT, THE DEFENDANT HAS THE BURDEN OF RAISING A TRIABLE FACT ISSUE

Plaintiffs in negligence cases make far fewer motions for summary judgment than do defendants. When a plaintiff does move for summary judgment, the plaintiff must show that there are no fact issues standing in the way of judgment. This is a high standard to meet because a fact issue almost always exists as to whether the defendant's conduct constituted negligence.

**CASE 17. The blind-sided pedestrian: The plaintiff's own conduct may create a triable fact issue.** In the next case, a driver looking for a parking spot drove backwards in the wrong direction on a one-way street. He hit a pedestrian who was jaywalking. The pedestrian's theory of the case was that the driver was negligent in that he was driving backwards in the wrong direction on a one-way street. When the pedestrian moved for summary judgment, the driver argued that the pedestrian's own conduct partially caused his injury.

**VICTOR PAREJA, plaintiff, v. WILLIAM H. BROWN, defendant.**
795 N.Y.Supp.2d 666 (2d Dep't 2005)

**The Court:** The plaintiff Victor Pareja, a pedestrian, attempted to cross a street at a point other than an intersection or a crosswalk, and was struck by the left side-view mirror of the defendant William H. Brown's vehicle, which was going in reverse in order to locate a parking spot.

Pareja alleged that he attempted to cross the street in the middle of the block, and that there was a vehicle parked to the right of him and another vehicle parked to the left of him. Right before impact, Pareja was staring at a building across the street which was under construction, and he did not see the defendant's vehicle. Brown alleged that he was looking at his rear-view and side-view mirrors as he backed up and did not see Pareja before the impact.

Under the circumstance, the trial court properly denied Pareja's motion for summary judgment on the issue of liability.[11] Pareja failed to submit evidence sufficient to establish as a matter of law that Brown's alleged negligence in the operation of his vehicle was the sole proximate cause of the accident.

Triable issues of fact exist as to whether Pareja contributed to the accident by failing to exercise due care in crossing the street at a point other than an intersection or a crosswalk, and whether Brown contributed to the accident by failing to exercise due care in operating his vehicle.

### ANALYSIS

The opinion does not state whether the pedestrian was walking forward when hit, but we do know that he was hit by the driver-side mirror which is closer to the front of the vehicle. This means that more than half of the backward moving vehicle had passed the pedestrian before he was hit. From that fact it might be inferred that the pedestrian was also not paying attention. The defendant thus established a triable fact issue concerning the plaintiff's own negligence.

**CASE 18. The pedestrian in the crosswalk: Sometimes even a plaintiff may win summary judgment.** In this next case a New York City bus ran down the plaintiff who was walking with the light in a crosswalk. The plaintiff moved for summary judgment which the court granted.

**MICHAEL HOEY, plaintiff, v. CITY OF NEW YORK, defendant.**
813 N.Y.Supp.2d 533 (2d Dep't 2006)

**The Court:** The plaintiff Michael Hoey was struck by a bus owned by the defendant New York City Transit Authority while Hoey was crossing the street in a crosswalk with the pedestrian signal in his favor. The

---

11. A motion for summary judgment on liability addresses only the defendant's liability, not the question of damages. The motion leaves for a later stage in the trial the issue of damages. If the plaintiff wins the motion, the trial will continue, but the only issue will be the amount of damages. [Ed.]

defendant acknowledged that Hoey was in the crosswalk and had the right of way, but argued that a triable issue of fact existed as to whether Hoey was comparatively negligent.

We agree with the trial court that Hoey established his entitlement to summary judgment against the defendant. Hoey's deposition testimony that at the time of the accident he was looking straight ahead, observing vehicles making right-hand turns onto the street he was crossing, was corroborated by the deposition testimony of a nonparty witness to the accident. This explanation for not having seen the bus before it struck him was sufficient to establish a lack of carelessness on his part and thus established his entitlement to summary judgment on the issue of liability against the defendant. In opposition, the defendant failed to raise a triable issue of fact.

### ANALYSIS

The Transit Authority argued in its attempt to create a triable issue that a reasonable pedestrian should be on the lookout for danger, even when crossing with the light. This was sound advice, but it was not sufficient to deny Hoey his summary judgment.

# CHAPTER 7

# Presumptions

## A. A PRESUMPTION MAY SUPPORT A PRIMA FACIE CASE

A presumption is a legal conclusion drawn from a particular fact or other evidence which is taken as true unless and until the truth of that legal conclusion is disproved.

A familiar example of a presumption is that a person accused of a crime is presumed innocent until proven guilty. The presumption of innocence allocates the burdens of proof between the accused and the prosecutor. The accused in whose favor the presumption works need not do anything, while his or her opponent, the prosecutor, has the burden of producing evidence sufficient to defeat the presumption of innocence. The accused can sit silently and offer no evidence, yet the accused may still win if the prosecutor fails to overcome the presumption by proving guilt beyond a reasonable doubt.

A presumption can be a quality ascribed to a person, to a relationship, or to a description of a thing or event, that is legally controlling unless it is proven to a legal satisfaction not to be true. Here are additional examples of presumptions:

- A person missing for seven years is presumed dead for such matters as marriage and ownership of property. The foundation fact that establishes the presumption is that the person has been missing for seven years; the presumed conclusion is that the person is legally dead.
- If a couple has gone through a marriage ceremony, their marriage is presumed in law to be valid.
- A child under the age of four is presumed incapable of negligent conduct even though the child can still cause injury to another. The foundational fact is the child's age; the presumption is that the child cannot be legally negligent.

The common thread to these presumptions is that the party against whom they work (i.e., the party opposing the presumption) must respond or suffer the consequence of the presumption becoming legally conclusive. This is how presumptions allocate burdens of proof.

Of the presumptions above, three are rebuttable presumptions: the person accused of a crime, the person missing for seven years, and the couple who went through the marriage ceremony. A party seeking to oppose any of these presumptions has to refute the presumption by producing contrary evidence of sufficient persuasiveness to overcome the presumption.

But not all presumptions are rebuttable. Some are conclusive. The last example concerning the child less than four years of age is not rebuttable. It is a conclusive presumption. The person opposing the presumption is not given the opportunity to rebut the presumption.

Common law judges developed presumptions in order to ease the burden of proof in repetitive situations where logic and experience supported the presumption, and where, without the presumption, unfairness or injustice would have resulted. Not all presumptions survive. In Charles Dickens' *Oliver Twist*, Mr. Bumble, in Chapter 51, is told that the law presumes that a husband is in control of his wife's actions. Mr. Bumble replies that if the law supposes that, "the law is a ass, a idiot," (sic) a sentiment with which our law has come to agree.

A presumption may be sufficient to establish a prima facie case. The following three cases demonstrate the impact of a presumption on a burden of proof, the requirement to respond, and summary judgment.

**CASE 19. A rear-end collision: The trailing driver is presumed to be negligent.** Plaintiff Virginia Dileo was riding in the front passenger seat of the leading car. The defendant, Marc B. Greenstein, the driver of the trailing car, rammed the rear end of the car in which Dileo was seated. Dileo sued Greenstein, alleging negligence. Dileo, the plaintiff, relied on the presumption that when a trailing driver rams the rear end of the leading car, the trailing driver is presumed to be negligent. The trailing driver, the party opposing the presumption, claimed that the lead car stopped short, but failed to produce supporting evidence. In that situation the presumption was sufficient to compel summary judgment in favor of the plaintiff on liability.

---

**VIRGINIA DILEO, plaintiff, v. MARC B. GREENSTEIN, defendant.**
722 N.Y.Supp.2d 259 (2d Dep't 2001)

**The Court:** A rear-end collision with a stopped vehicle establishes prima facie that the driver of the moving vehicle was negligent and imposes a duty on him or her to explain how the accident occurred. If the operator of the moving vehicle cannot come forward with any evidence to rebut the inference of negligence, the driver of the lead vehicle may properly be awarded judgment as a matter of law.

A claim by the trailing driver that the lead vehicle made a sudden stop is insufficient to rebut the presumption of negligence. The trial court erred in denying Dileo's motion for summary judgment on the issue of liability, as the trailing driver's only claim was that the driver of the lead vehicle stopped short in heavy traffic.

[The appellate court sent the case back to the trial court for a trial limited to damages alone.]

### ANALYSIS

Reasonably careful drivers are supposed to be prepared for sudden stops by allowing sufficient space between cars. There are, however, nonnegligent reasons why a trailing driver might rear-end another car. The trailing car, for example, might have itself been hit from the rear and forced into the car in front.

The burden was initially on Dileo, the plaintiff passenger in the lead car, to establish that the trailing driver's conduct was negligent. Dileo met her burden by invoking the presumption, which forced the defendant to respond. The defendant testified in response that the lead car in which Dileo was riding stopped short. The bare claim by the trailing driver that the lead car stopped short is such a routine claim that the courts have adopted a rule that such a claim without additional, supporting proof is insufficient as a matter of law to overcome the presumption. In this case, there was no additional proof. As a result, the court, following precedent, ruled insufficient the bare testimony by the trailing driver that the front car stopped short. The judge as a result granted summary judgment to Dileo on liability, ruling that the trailing driver failed to produce evidence sufficient to overcome the presumption that he had been negligent.

**CASE 20.  Rear-ended on the drive to the nail salon: The defendant's response to a presumption may create a fact issue.** The presumption arising out of a rear-end collision, like most presumptions, can be rebutted. In this case the two high school teenage girls, on their way in separate cars to the nail salon, admitted that they were not paying attention. This led to a sudden stop and a rear-end collision. The defendant relied on this additional evidence to rebut the presumption.

**KELLY J. DANNER, plaintiff, v. JACKIE CAMPBELL, defendant.**
754 N.Y.Supp.2d 484 (4th Dep't 2003)

**The Court:** Plaintiff Kelly J. Danner commenced this action seeking damages for injuries that she sustained when the vehicle that she was driving was struck from behind by a vehicle driven by defendant

Jackie Campbell, who was following her to a nail salon from the high school they both attended.

It is well established that a rear-end collision with a stopped vehicle establishes a prima facie case of negligence on the part of the driver of the rear vehicle. The presumption of negligence imposes a duty of explanation with respect to the operation of the rear vehicle. A nonnegligent explanation for the collision, such as mechanical failure or the sudden and abrupt stop of the vehicle ahead, is sufficient to overcome the inference of negligence and preclude the award of summary judgment.

Here plaintiff Danner, the driver of the lead car, met her initial burden of the motion by establishing that her vehicle was rear-ended by the vehicle driven by defendant Campbell. Campbell, however, raised an issue of fact by submitting the deposition testimony of plaintiff Danner, the lead driver, in which Danner stated that because she was looking at the street signs, she did not see a vehicle move into the lane directly in front of her vehicle. Plaintiff Danner admitted that she slammed on her brakes to avoid hitting that vehicle, and that is when the vehicle driven by defendant Campbell rear-ended her vehicle.

We conclude that defendant Campbell thereby offered a nonnegligent explanation for the collision, rendering summary judgment in favor of plaintiff inappropriate.

[The appellate division sent the case back to the trial court for trial.]

### ANALYSIS

The court in this opinion stated that once plaintiff Danner testified that she was rear-ended by the defendant Campbell, Danner had met her burden; this was shorthand for saying that Danner had established a prima facie case that Campbell was negligent based on the presumption that the trailing driver was negligent.

The court then stated that the presumption "imposes a duty of explanation" on the defendant. This meant that, unless the trailing driver rebutted the presumption with a credible explanation supported by evidence, the presumption would not only be prima facie, it would be conclusive.

Campbell, the trailing driver, responded by testifying that the lead car stopped short, but, unlike the first case above, she was able to produce supporting evidence. That evidence came in the form of the lead driver's own testimony given in a post-accident deposition to the effect that she, as lead driver, was not paying attention, and that it was the sudden realization that she was about to hit a car that caused her to slam on the brakes and stop suddenly. The presumption in favor of the lead driver did not disappear but remained in the case for the jury to consider along with the other testimony. If the jury credits the trailing driver's explanation, the plaintiff will lose despite initially benefitting from the presumption.

REAR END
COLLISION

**CASE 21. Rear-ended in a chain accident: The defendant's response may defeat the presumption entirely.** In this three-car collision, the plaintiff in the lead car invoked the presumption against the middle car that rear-ended it, but the presumption was not enough when the middle car's evidence conclusively showed that it was shoved into the plaintiff's car.

---

**CAROL ANDERSON, plaintiff, v. EILEEN RYDER, CAMILLE STANISLAUS, AND BERNADETTE HARRIS, defendants.**
739 N.Y.S. 2d 195 (2d Dep't 2002)

**The Court:** This action grew out of a three-vehicle collision that occurred at the intersection of Eastern Parkway and Atlantic Avenue in Brooklyn. A vehicle owned by Eileen Ryder and operated by Barbara Ryder hit the rear of a vehicle owned by Camille Stanislaus and operated by Bernadette Louis Harris. The impact propelled the Stanislaus vehicle into the vehicle in front of it, owned and operated by Carol Anderson, the plaintiff. In support of their motion for summary judgment, the defendants Stanislaus and Harris established that their vehicle, after coming to a complete stop, was struck in the rear by the vehicle operated by the defendant Ryder. Anderson sued the drivers of both vehicles. The trial court denied the motion for summary judgment by Stanislaus and Harris, the owner and driver of the middle vehicle. We reverse.

It is well settled that a rear-end collision with a stopped vehicle creates a prima facie case of liability with respect to the operator of the moving vehicle unless the operator of the moving vehicle can come forward with an adequate, nonnegligent explanation for the accident.

Under these circumstances, the defendants Stanislaus and Harris provided a nonnegligent reason for hitting the rear of Anderson's vehicle. The fact that Anderson testified that she heard and felt only one impact does not raise a triable issue of fact as to the sequence of impacts involved in the accident, and the defendants Stanislaus and Harris were entitled to summary judgment dismissing Anderson's claim against them.

### ANALYSIS

In this case the evidence that the middle car was shoved into the lead car was so persuasive that the presumption lost even its capacity to create a triable issue. The court accordingly granted the middle car summary judgment dismissing the lead car's claim against it. The lead car, of course, still has her claim against the third car that started the chain, and there the presumption is still alive.

# CHAPTER 8

# Burden and Verdicts

In litigating a tort case the plaintiff has the initial burden of producing proof sufficient to establish a prima facie case as explained in Chapter 5. The plaintiff also has the burden of ultimate persuasion, which is also called the burden of proof. The "burden" in these phrases is the risk of nonpersuasion.

## A. THE BURDEN OF PERSUASION IS ON THE PLAINTIFF

The risk of nonpersuasion in a negligence case is on the plaintiff, and that burden never shifts. Judge Lemuel Shaw of Massachusetts, a judge who during the nineteenth century wrote several influential tort opinions, clarified the plaintiff's burden in *Brown v. Kendall*, the leading American negligence decision that, because of its importance, appears or is cited in every torts casebook. Judge Shaw wrote the following:

> Those facts which are essential to enable the plaintiff to recover, he takes the burden of proving. The evidence may be offered by the plaintiff or defendant; the question of due care, or want of care, may be essentially connected with the main facts, and arise from the same proof; but the effect of the rule, as to the burden of proof, is this, that when the proof is all in, and before the jury, from whatever side it comes, and whether directly proved, or inferred from circumstances ... unless it also appears to the satisfaction of the jury, that the defendant [was negligent], the plaintiff fails to sustain the burden of proof and is not entitled to recover.[12]

The burden of proof remains with the plaintiff throughout the litigation, even though the rhythm of litigation produces a stroke and counterstroke that appears to and sometimes actually causes the shift of a particularly evidentiary burden from one party to the other. The plaintiff, for example, may allege

---

12. Brown v. Kendall, 60 Mass. 292, 298 (1850).

sufficient facts to meet its burden of a prima facie case, but then the defendant in response may meet its burden to establish a prima facie defense that, if unanswered by the plaintiff, will result in a victory for the defendant and the dismissal of the plaintiff's case.

While this may seem confusing, the application of burden of proof in a particular case becomes clear by restating the plaintiff's theory of the case, and then identifying the evidence needed to support that theory. In the process you will almost automatically set out the burden correctly.

## B. THE PLAINTIFF MUST CARRY ITS BURDEN OF PERSUASION BY A PREPONDERANCE OF THE EVIDENCE

At the conclusion of the presentation of evidence, when both sides have rested, the lawyers give their final summations. It is then that the judge, through his or her instructions, gives directions to the members of the jury on how to resolve the fact issues raised by the evidence.

The core of the judge's instructions or charge to the jury is a discussion of the standard by which the jury is to make its findings. In a tort trial the standard is the preponderance of the evidence. Here is an example of a judge's prepared charge to the jury setting forth the standard by which the jury is to decide whether the plaintiff has met its burden of proof.[13]

> The burden of proof rests on the plaintiff. That means that the truth of the plaintiff's claim must be established by a fair preponderance of the credible evidence. The credible evidence means the testimony or exhibits that you [the members of the jury] find to be worthy to be believed.
>
> A preponderance of the evidence means the greater part of such evidence. That does not mean the greater number of witnesses or the greater length of time taken by either side. The phrase a preponderance of the evidence refers to the quality of the evidence, that is, its convincing quality, the weight and the effect that it has on your minds. The law requires that in order for the plaintiff to prevail on a claim, the evidence that supports (his, her) claim must appeal to you as more nearly representing what took place than the evidence opposed to (his, her) claim. If it does not, or if it weighs so evenly that you are unable to say that there is a preponderance on either side, then you must decide the question in favor of the defendant. It is only if the evidence favoring the

---

13. Reprinted from *New York Jury Instructions—Civil* (3rd ed.), PJI 1-23, with the permission of Thomson Reuters.

plaintiff's claim outweighs the evidence opposed to it that you can find in favor of the plaintiff.

Another way of saying this is that the jury must find that the plaintiff's claim is to be established as more likely than not.

## C. THE JURY RESOLVES FACT ISSUES BY ITS VERDICT

**CASE 22. The youth who tried to outrun a subway train: Judges are bound by a jury's verdict if that verdict is supported by the evidence.** In this case a subway train struck an inebriated 18-year-old youth who, late at night, wandered onto the subway tracks. When the youth realized that a train was approaching he tried to outrun the train. The train won, and the youth sued the Transit Authority on the theory that the train operator should have seen him and stopped in time. The jury found the Transit Authority liable, and assigned 25 percent of the fault to the Transit Authority and 75 percent of the fault to the youth's own reckless conduct. The Transit Authority appealed.

On appeal, the appellate court split. Three judges voted to uphold the verdict, and two, in dissent, voted to overturn it.

**JUAN ALEJANDRO SOTO, plaintiff, v. NEW YORK CITY TRANSIT AUTH., defendant.**
800 N.Y.Supp.2d 419 (2d Dep't 2005)

**The Court (three-judge majority):** After an evening of drinking with friends, plaintiff Soto, then 18 years old, and three friends descended the platform at the 33rd Street subway station in Queens and walked on the three-foot-wide catwalk next to the train tracks because they believed the northbound track of the Number 7 train between the 33rd Street and 40th Street stations was not in service. A train approached from behind and struck Soto who testified that he was running at a speed he estimated as between seven and eight miles per hour. Soto sustained serious injuries.

We agree with Soto's contention on this appeal that the jury's verdict in his favor was supported by legally sufficient evidence.[14] Soto estimated his running speed based on his two years' experience before the accident of regularly running on a treadmill. Because Soto's estimate was based on his personal knowledge and experience as a runner, it was appropriate for his expert witness to use Soto's estimate in his

---

14. "Legally sufficient evidence" in this context means that the evidence admitted at trial was, however minimal, sufficient to support the verdict. [Ed.]

calculations. We disagree with the dissent's conclusion that Soto's testimony and the expert's opinion concerning Soto's running speed were based on pure speculation. The factual dispute arising from Soto's estimate of his running speed was a matter for the jury's resolution.

Further, the disagreement between the parties' experts regarding the distance at which the train operator should have seen Soto and his friends was also a matter for the jury that heard and observed the experts' testimony; the jury's resolution of conflicting expert testimony is entitled to great weight. The jury's finding that the defendant New York City Transit Authority train operator could have avoided the accident was supported by legally sufficient evidence.

**The Dissent (two-judge minority):** The trial court erred in allowing Soto to testify regarding his estimate of his running speed. He testified that in the past he ran 50 to 100 times on a treadmill in a gym. Thus, according to Soto, he knew that he could run seven to eight miles per hour, and that he was running in front of the train at that speed on the evening of the accident. The trial court further erred in permitting Soto's expert to opine, based on the foregoing testimony, that the train operator could have stopped the train 51 feet away from Soto, if Soto was running at eight miles an hour, and 37 feet away if he was running at seven miles per hour.

Soto's testimony and the expert's opinion were based on pure speculation and conjecture. There was absolutely no foundation to establish that the equipment allegedly previously utilized by Soto at the gym was, in fact, properly calibrated to reflect an accurate speed-reading. Further, running conditions on a treadmill in a gym setting are entirely different from those presented at the time of the subject incident.

### ANALYSIS

Whether the train operator could stop in time (Soto's theory of the case) was not a question susceptible to a certain answer no matter how wise the jury or clear the testimony. It was a matter of credibility and judgment. The trial judge as gatekeeper decided that Soto had introduced sufficient evidence to establish a prima facie case and to allow the jury to resolve the fact issues. In the opinion above, three middle-level appellate judges agreed with the trial judge's decision, and two disagreed.

This case has had a lengthy history. At a first trial, the jury assigned 100 percent of the fault to the New York City Transit Authority. The Appellate Division reversed that judgment, ruling that the verdict was contrary to the evidence, and the case was retried. At the second trial the jury found plaintiff Soto 75 percent at fault, the Transit Authority only 25 percent at fault, and awarded $5 million to Soto who had lost both legs below the knees in the accident. Deducting 75 percent (the portion of the award that the jury found was Soto's own fault), the verdict still netted Soto over $1.4 million (with interest). The Transit Authority appealed. The decision above is the Appellate Division's opinion upholding the jury's verdict in the second trial.

In a final attempt to overturn the jury's verdict, the Transit Authority appealed to the New York Court of Appeals, the state's highest court. The Court of Appeals rejected the appeal and affirmed the Appellate Division but did so in yet another split decision. Four judges voted to affirm (in favor of Soto), and three voted to reverse. The three judges who voted to reverse felt that Soto's recklessness was so pronounced that the jury could not have rationally assigned even 25 percent of the fault to the Transit Authority. *Soto v. New York City Transit Authority*, 813 N.Y.Supp.2d 701 (N.Y. 2006).

The decision by the Court of Appeals allowing the verdict to stand caused a storm of protest. The *New York Daily News* ran a front-page story with a three-inch-high headline: "DRUNK JUSTICE: Boozed-up guy tries to outrun train, loses legs, then wins $1.4 M." In a companion editorial, the *New York Daily News* called the decision "looney" and the judges who voted to affirm the verdict "off their rockers" (*New York Daily News*, March 25, 2006, pp. 1, 3, and 24. © New York Daily, News, L.P., used with permission).

Counting up the judicial votes, eight judges voted to sustain the jury's verdict for Soto and five voted with the Transit Authority. The jury, of course, was unanimous on the 75/25 split. This tells you a lot about the deference judges regularly, but not always, give to jury verdicts.

**CASE 23. The car with two backseat drivers: The jury resolves the dispute between witnesses.** A two-vehicle accident resulted in the death of Kevin L. Shea who was driving alone in his car. The executor of Shea's estate sued but found himself confronted with the unexpected circumstances that the two occupants of the other car in the accident were both found in the back seat. Each denied that he had been the driver. This odd circumstance presented the plaintiff with the problem of proving which of the two "backseat passengers" had actually driven the second car.

The jury's verdict resolved which of the two had been the driver. The one identified as the driver appealed.

THE CAR WITH TWO BACK-SEAT DRIVERS

**JAMES SHEA, AS EXECUTOR OF THE ESTATE OF KEVIN L. SHEA, DECEASED, plaintiff, v. ROBERT H. MAZZA, II AND JEFFREY C. MCFALL, defendants.**
762 N.Y.Supp.2d 221 (4th Dep't 2003)

**The Court:** Robert H. Mazza was involved in a collision while traveling in a vehicle with Jeffrey C. McFall. The vehicle, which was owned by McFall, struck a pickup truck driven by Kevin L. Shea, the plaintiff who is deceased. When other motorists stopped to provide assistance, they discovered Mazza and McFall in the backseat of the vehicle. No eyewitness could place Mazza or McFall in the driver's seat before or after the accident, and there was conflicting evidence concerning the identity of the driver.

The jury returned a verdict finding that Mazza was the driver at the time of the accident. Mazza moved for judgment in his favor notwithstanding the verdict or, alternatively, to set aside the verdict as against the weight of the evidence and for a new trial. The trial court judge granted Mazza judgment notwithstanding the verdict and dismissed all claims against him, determining as a matter of law that McFall was the driver of the vehicle at the time of the accident.

We conclude that the jury verdict must be reinstated. The sole issue at trial was the identity of the driver at the time of the accident. Given the conflicting testimony on that issue, we conclude that the jury verdict that Mazza was the driver is supported by sufficient evidence (i.e., there is a valid line of reasoning and permissible inferences that could lead rational persons to the conclusion reached by the jury based on the evidence at the trial), and thus the court erred in granting Mazza judgment notwithstanding the verdict.

Furthermore, contrary to the contention of Mazza, the jury verdict finding that he was the driver of the vehicle at the time of the accident is not against the weight of the evidence (i.e., it cannot be said that the jury verdict could not have been reached on any fair interpretation of the evidence), and thus he is not entitled to a new trial.[15]

It is hereby ordered that the jury verdict be reinstated.

---

15. This sentence is difficult to understand because of the repeated use of the negative. It would have been easier to understand if it had read as follows:

> "Mazza contends that the jury's verdict should be overturned. He argues that the verdict is not reasonably supported by the weight of the evidence. But, in the judgment of this court, the jury's verdict was based on a fair interpretation of the evidence. As a result the verdict as reported by the jury stands: there will be no new trial." [Ed.]

### ANALYSIS

The jury resolved the dispute as to who was driving the car, not to a certainty, but as a matter of probability. More likely than not, the driver was Mazza.

Problems in identifying the defendant occur more often than one would suppose. For example, a speeding black SUV drives another car off the road and into a tree. The black SUV keeps going. All the victim knows was that it was a black SUV. The plaintiff has the burden of producing a prima facie case with respect to every element of the plaintiff's theory, including the identity of the defendant. Unless the victim can identify the driver or owner of the SUV, the victim is simply out of luck.

**CASE 24. The shallow dive into the pool: A court may review a jury verdict for logical consistency.** In this case a young man dove or jumped into a public swimming pool and was injured. Although he walked out of the pool unaided, he suffered a spinal injury that left him a quadriplegic. He sued New York City. The verdict reached by the jury, however, gave inconsistent answers to specific questions posed to them by the judge. As a result the trial judge rejected the verdict.

**EDWARD PENA, plaintiff, v. CITY OF NEW YORK, defendant.**
N.Y.L.J., p. 29 (Nov. 25, 1997) (Sup. Ct. N.Y.Cty.)

**The Court:** This is a motion by the defendant City of New York to set aside the verdict as a matter of law. The facts that brought the parties to court occurred on October 12, 1991, at about noon. Plaintiff Edward Pena either dove or jumped into a three-and-one-half-foot-deep swimming pool, owned and maintained by defendant City of New York. He sustained fractures of the cervical spine at the C-4 and C-5 levels. Pena was able to walk to the side of the pool and climb onto the deck with the assistance of his friends. Giulina Cardillo, a New York City lifeguard, then rendered assistance. Pena was rendered a quadriplegic as a result.

At trial Pena offered two theories of negligence by the City. Both theories are based on the premise that the fractures caused by his entry into the pool resulted only in quadriparesis, a temporary paralysis of the upper and lower extremities, which was not permanent as evidenced by his ability to walk out of the pool. Pena for his first theory argued that the lifeguard negligently moved Pena's head and neck from side to side, instead of immobilizing it, transecting the spinal cord and rendering him a complete quadriplegic.

In the alternative, Pena argued that the lifeguard was not constant and diligent in scanning and surveying the area of the pool for which she was responsible. As a result, she failed to recognize the problem and render immediate attention to Pena while he was still in the pool. Pena further argues that had immediate assistance been rendered in the pool, his neck would have been stabilized, a spine board applied, and the quadriplegia avoided.

The jury verdict sheet contained questions as to both theories and as to damages. The jurors replied "no" on the issue of whether the lifeguard moved Pena's head or neck, and therefore did not have to answer the second question as to whether this aggravated Pena's initial injuries.

In response to question number 3, the jury determined that the City was negligent, and to question number 4 that said negligence was a substantial factor in causing Pena's accident.

The jury allocated 15% of the liability to the City and 85% to Pena. An award of $900,000 was made for past pain and suffering; $85,000 for future medical expenses for 17 years; $595,000 for future custodial expenses for 3 years; $85,000 for future transportation cost for 1 year; and $0 for future pain and suffering.

The trial testimony concerning the lifeguard's responsibility to continually scan and survey the pool, and the time it took for a lifeguard to get to Pena, may be some evidence of negligence. However, there was absolutely no testimony, expert or otherwise, that such negligence worsened the injuries Pena suffered when he entered the pool. In other words, there was no credible evidence that the severity of Pena's injuries could have been avoided with prompt action by the lifeguard. Viewing all of the evidence in a manner most favorable to Pena, this court can find no valid line of reasoning and permissible inferences that could possibly lead rational men to the conclusion reached by the jury on the basis of the evidence presented at trial.

Accordingly, the motion of the City of New York, for an order setting aside the verdict and for judgment as a matter of law in its favor, is granted.

### ANALYSIS

Pena had the burden of persuading the jury that, more likely than not, the lifeguard's negligence caused him to become a quadriplegic. The jury's verdict, however, eliminated the negligence of the lifeguard as a possibility.

Pena's first theory was that the lifeguard, in treating him, injured his spine. The jury found that this did not happen. His second theory was that the lifeguard failed to respond quickly enough while Pena was still in the pool. Here the jury agreed that the lifeguard did not respond quickly.

But the victim walked out of the pool. The plaintiff had to show that, more likely than not, the lifeguard's failure to come to his aid while he was in the pool caused his spinal injury. Because the victim walked out of the pool, the negligence proven could not have possibly caused the paralysis injury. As the court stated, "there was no credible evidence that the severity of Pena's injuries could have been avoided with prompt action by the lifeguard" while the victim was still in the pool. As a result, the jury could not find by a preponderance of the evidence that the City was even 25 percent responsible.

# CHAPTER 9

# Appellate Issues

## A. A JUDICIAL OPINION DECIDES DISPUTES

Appellate court opinions are what law students almost exclusively read in a torts class. Some appellate court opinions may be read for enjoyment, but the primary purpose for reading appellate court opinions is utilitarian: to learn how law is actually applied by judges.

A judicial opinion can best be understood by identifying the dispute to which the opinion is directed. The first task of the lawyer is to identify the dispute. That dispute, when it is in an appellate court, is the "appellate issue," and it is the appellate issue that provides the structure on which the appellate court opinion hangs.

An appellate issue has three characteristics:

1. *The appellate issue is always a question.* Often the question is assumed, abbreviated, or not directly stated in the opinion, but it is there nonetheless.
2. *The question that is the appellate issue is always framed as an issue of law.* Appellate courts generally only decide legal questions. A proper appellate issue must be framed as a question of law and not a question of fact.
3. *The issue of law is always directed at a ruling by the lower court judge.* The form of an appeal is framed as a challenge to a ruling or rulings of law by the lower court judge. An appellant's argument on appeal is that the lower court judge made an error of law, and that the appellate court should correct that error.

It is helpful when stating the issue on appeal to use the same formula that appellate lawyers generally use in their appellate briefs. Here is the formula:

DID THE TRIAL COURT

ERR

WHEN IT RULED THAT

[SPECIFY THE RULING ALLEGED TO BE AN ERROR]?

In the first case in this book, the snow tuber's dismount at page 15, the defendant ski area appealed the trial court's denial of its motion for summary judgment. The ski area argued that Cory Huneau, the injured plaintiff-snow-tuber, assumed the risk of injury when he voluntarily participated in snow tubing. The trial judge, however, ruled that Huneau had established a prima facie case on whether the ski area's conduct had unreasonably increased the risk to Huneau beyond the ordinary risks of snow tubing. The appellate question addressed on the ski area's appeal might have been stated as follows:

> Did the trial court err when, in denying the ski area's motion for summary judgment, it ruled that there were triable issues as to whether the ski area's conduct unreasonably increased the risk to Huneau beyond the ordinary risks of snow tubing?

Lawyers often shorten the appellate issue by simply stating:

> Did the trial court err when it denied the defendant's motion for summary judgment?

or

> Did the trial court err when it ruled that the plaintiff had established a triable issue requiring a trial?

Lawyers may also put the question in a positive form to give the question a more argumentative tone. For example, the ski area might eliminate the phrase "Did the court err," and assert the same thought as a declarative statement:

> The ski area was entitled to summary judgment.

or

> The plaintiff failed to establish a prima facie case that the ski area was liable for his injury.

## B. AN APPELLATE ISSUE IS ALWAYS A QUESTION

**CASE 25.  The body in the road: Whether a triable fact issue exists is an issue of law.** In this case James Pawlukiewicz, a passenger in a car involved in a highway collision, was ejected from the car and lay in the middle of the road. Kent S. Rydberg, the defendant, was the driver in a trailing car that arrived at the scene moments after the accident. Rydberg attempted to thread his way between the two damaged cars and, in the process, ran over Pawlukiewicz lying prone in the roadway. Rydberg moved for summary judgment, arguing that he was confronted with an emergency situation and, because of the emergency, should be excused from liability as a matter of law for striking Pawlukiewicz. The trial judge denied the defendant's motion.

Defendant Rydberg appealed, claiming that the judge should have granted his motion for summary judgment. The dispute between the parties concerned whether Rydberg was actually confronted with an emergency. The appellate issue was whether the trial judge erred when he ruled that Rydberg failed to establish that the existence of an emergency was of sufficient magnitude that Rydberg should be relieved of liability.

**JAMES PAWLUKIEWICZ, plaintiff, v. MARIE N. BOISSON AND KENT S. RYDBERG, defendants.**
712 N.Y.Supp.2d 634 (2d Dep't 2000)

**The Court:** The plaintiff James Pawlukiewicz was a passenger in a vehicle driven by Patrick Taylor which crossed over into the oncoming lane of traffic and collided with an oncoming vehicle driven by Ingver A. Nelson. Plaintiff Pawlukiewicz was ejected from Taylor's vehicle in which he was riding. The defendant Kent S. Rydberg, who was driving behind the Nelson vehicle, drove through a space that opened up between the Taylor and the Nelson vehicles, and his vehicle came into contact with Pawlukiewicz, who was then in Rydberg's path of travel.

Rydberg moved for summary judgment, dismissing the complaint insofar as asserted against him based on the emergency doctrine. Rydberg argued that the accident created an emergency situation, and that his actions were reasonable under the circumstances. We affirm the trial court's refusal to dismiss plaintiff Pawlukiewicz's complaint.

The emergency doctrine recognizes that when an actor is faced with a sudden and unexpected circumstance not of his or her own making, which leaves little or no time for thought, deliberation, or consideration, or causes the actor to be reasonably so disturbed that the actor must make a speedy decision without weighing alternative courses of conduct, the actor may not be held negligent if the actions taken are reasonable and prudent in the emergency context, even if it later appears that the actor made a wrong decision.

This is not to say that an emergency automatically absolves one from liability for his or her conduct. The standard then still remains that of a reasonable man under the given circumstances, except that the circumstances have changed. Whether Rydberg had little or no time for thought, deliberation, or consideration before coming upon the accident scene and allegedly striking Pawlukiewicz, or was unable to weigh alternative courses of conduct before acting, requires consideration of, inter alia, the distance and speed at which Rydberg chose to follow the Nelson vehicle.

By statute, Rydberg was obliged to maintain a reasonable and prudent distance from the Nelson vehicle, with due regard for traffic and weather conditions. Further, he was obliged to see that which he should have seen with the proper use of his senses. Thus, a reasonable jury could conclude that the emergency doctrine is not applicable.

Further, assuming that the emergency doctrine is applicable, Rydberg's motion was still properly denied. In various sworn statements, Rydberg asserted that at the time of the collision he was traveling in a four-wheel-drive vehicle at a speed of approximately 15 miles per hour and was two to three car lengths behind the Nelson vehicle. Assuming that these allegations are credited, it cannot be said, as a matter of law, that a reasonable jury could not conclude that Rydberg's failure or inability to stop or turn his vehicle before coming upon the accident scene and allegedly coming into contact with Pawlukiewicz was unreasonable, even under emergency circumstances.

In sum, whether Rydberg was negligent and, if so, whether such negligence was a proximate cause of the injuries alleged, present issues of fact for the jury.

### ANALYSIS

The appellate court did not explicitly state an appellate issue, but it was present nonetheless. The way to discover the appellate issue is to identify the legal dispute that generated the appeal.

Here the dispute related to whether the defendant Rydberg had established that he was confronted with an emergency such that a jury would be compelled to conclude that he was not liable for running over Pawlukiewicz. Pawlukiewicz, the injured plaintiff, disputed both the extent of the emergency and Rydberg's response to it. The appellate issue arising from this dispute focused on the trial judge's ruling denying Rydberg's motion for summary judgment. The appellate issue might variously have been stated as follows:

- Did the trial court err when it denied Rydberg's motion for summary judgment?
- Did the trial court err when it ruled that there were triable fact issues that required resolution by the jury?
- Did the trial court err when it ruled that the jury will have to resolve the question of whether Rydberg acted reasonably?
- Did the trial court err when it defined the emergency doctrine as requiring a showing by Rydberg that he had little or no time for thought, deliberation, or consideration or was unable to weigh alternative courses of conduct before acting?

By identifying the appellate question, you will begin to comprehend the structure and import of the appellate decision.

## C. AN APPELLATE ISSUE ALWAYS ADDRESSES AN ISSUE OF LAW

**CASE 26. The man who dropped an automobile on his finger: Whether a jury verdict is supported by the evidence is an issue of law.** In this case the plaintiff was injured while trying to lift up an automobile that had become entangled with a metal pipe in a parking lot. The defendant was the owner of the parking lot. The trial court jury found the parking lot owner 100 percent responsible and awarded damages of $365,000 to the injured plaintiff. The dispute on appeal was whether the judge was correct in accepting the jury's verdict placing 100 percent of the fault on the parking lot owner. The appellate issue was whether the trial judge erred in making that ruling.

**JOHN W. WERNER, plaintiff, v. ELLEN RITTER, defendant.**
723 N.Y.Supp.2d 216 (2d Dep't 2001)

**The Court:** John W. Werner [the car owner] was injured when he and a coworker attempted to extricate Werner's vehicle, which had become lodged on a metal pipe in the parking lot owned by Ellen Ritter. In attempting to move the vehicle, Werner placed his hand beneath the bumper of the vehicle and tried to lift it over the pipe while the coworker drove the vehicle off of the pipe. As the vehicle moved, Werner's finger became wedged between the metal pipe and the car bumper.

On these facts, the jury's finding that Werner was not negligent was against the weight of the evidence. No fair interpretation of the evidence supports the finding that Werner, who elected to lift the front bumper while his coworker reversed the car, was free from negligence.

Ordered that the judgment is reversed, on the facts, and the matter remanded to the trial court for a new trial.

### ANALYSIS

The parking lot owner challenged the jury's verdict as inconsistent with the evidence and asked the trial judge to set the jury's verdict aside. The trial judge refused, and the parking lot owner appealed. The appellant parking lot owner argued that the jury ignored the evidence that the plaintiff voluntarily attempted to lift up a moving car, and that, under comparative fault, some portion of the cost of the injury had to be placed on him for that negligent conduct. The appellate court, to resolve this dispute, evaluated the evidence but did so within the context of an appellate issue framed in legal terms. The appellate issue was

Did the trial judge err in refusing to set aside the jury's verdict as against the weight of the evidence?

or

The jury's verdict placing 100 percent of the fault on the defendant was not supported by the evidence.

## D. THE MEANING OF A STATUTE IS ALWAYS AN ISSUE OF LAW

**CASE 27. The bull that trampled the hunter: The interpretation of a statute is an issue of law.** In the following case a hunter hunting woodchucks in a farmer's cow pasture was trampled to death by the farmer's four-year-old Holstein bull. The hunter's survivors sued the farmer.

The farmer, in his defense, invoked a state statute that immunized landowners from liability for ordinary negligence when the landowner permitted people to use his land for recreational purposes. Such statutes, which are found in many states, encourage landowners to allow activities such as hunting, cross-country skiing, and camping by protecting landowner against tort liability. The party benefitting from immunity (the farmer in this case) was exempted from liability even though his conduct may have fallen below the standard of reasonable care. The trial court ruled that the statute did not immunize the farmer from liability for the hunter's death, and the farmer appealed.

The dispute between the parties concerned the interpretation of the statute. The appellate issue was whether the trial court erred when the judge ruled that the statute did not immunize the farmer from liability.

---

**ALAN C. OLSON, EXECUTOR FOR JOHN A. OLSON, plaintiff, v. CHRISTOPHER F. BRUNNER, defendant.**
689 N.Y.Supp.2d 833 (4th Dep't 1999)

**The Court:** Plaintiff, as executor of his father's will, commenced this wrongful death action after his father John A. Olson was fatally injured by a bull while hunting on defendant Brunner's dairy farm. The trial court erred in denying Brunner's motion for summary judgment, dismissing the complaint pursuant to General Obligation Law §9-103(1)(a).

Brunner owns a 207-acre dairy farm in North Java, New York. He has 60 Holstein cows and a four-year-old Holstein bull that run together for breeding purposes in a 70-acre pasture that is surrounded by a single strand of electrified barbed wire. Adjacent to the pasture is a cornfield.

For 10 years John A. Olson used the dairy farm to hunt. On the morning of September 4, 1996, Brunner gave Olson permission to hunt woodchucks on the premises. That evening Olson's body, which apparently had been trampled by the bull, was found beneath the electrified barbed-wire fence separating the pasture from the cornfield.

General Obligation Law §9-103(1)(a) grants immunity for ordinary negligence to landowners who permit members of the public to come on their property to engage in several enumerated recreational activities, including hunting. Such landowners owe no duty to keep their premises safe for hunters or to warn hunters of any hazardous condition on the landowner's premises when the hunter enters for hunting purposes.

We reject Olson's contention that the dairy farm is not suitable for hunting and that the statute therefore is not applicable. Although the statute was originally envisioned as applying to undeveloped or wilderness areas, there is nothing in the statute indicating that commercially used property should be treated differently from other property. While arguably a pasture with grazing cattle is not an appropriate area to hunt, suitability must be judged by viewing the property as it generally exists, not portions of it at some given time.

We also reject Olson's contention that because Brunner's alleged negligence concerns the keeping of a bull, the statute is not applicable. Although the statute does not immunize the affirmative negligence[16] of a landowner, the only arguable allegation of affirmative negligence is the allegation that Brunner allowed the bull to freely roam upon his property while knowing of Olson's presence. By all accounts, however, the bull was never free to roam outside the confines of a pasture that was enclosed by an electric fence. Brunner met his initial burden on his motion, and Olson did not submit any proof in opposition, raising a triable issue of fact whether the bull was roaming outside the confines of the enclosed pasture at the time of the accident.

The assumption of risk envisioned by the statute encompasses the risks associated with any hazardous condition, structure, or activity on the premises. As the quid pro quo for permission to hunt on Brunner's dairy farm, Olson assumed all the risks associated with the daily operation of that farm, including those risks associated with the pasturing of the bull and cows. To conclude otherwise would not be consistent with the intent of the statute, because it would effectively require landowners to alter their daily routine to accommodate hunters and to provide for their safety.

Olson's complaint is therefore dismissed.

### ANALYSIS

Judges, not juries, interpret statutes. The interpretation of a statute is a legal question. When the dispute is over the meaning of a statute, both parties have equivalent burdens. They both seek to persuade the judge that their interpretation is the correct one. Plaintiff Olsen made two arguments with respect to the statute: the statute did not apply to dairy farms generally, and that, even if it did, the statute did not apply with respect to bulls.

In his opinion the judge directly stated the appellate issue. It did so in the last sentence of the first paragraph of the opinion when it was stated that "The trial court erred in denying Brunner's motion for summary judgment dismissing the complaint pursuant to General Obligation Law §9-103(1)(a)." Add the word "Did" as the first word of the sentence, and change "erred" to "err," and you have the appellate issue as a question. The court could also have stated the appellate issue as follows:

---

16. "Affirmative negligence" in this sense means willful, malicious, or wanton acts on the part of the landowner. The plaintiff here is attempting to state a theory of the case that the landowner willfully endangered the hunter by allowing the bull to roam or by not properly alerting the hunter to the presence of the bull. [Ed.]

Did the trial court err when it denied the defendant's motion for summary judgment based on the immunity provision of General Obligation Law §9-103(1)(a)?

or

Did the trial court err when it ruled that the recreational immunity statute did not apply to an active dairy farm?

or

Did the trial court err when it ruled that the recreational immunity statute did not apply to conditions on the land that included the keeping of a breeding bull?

Because statutory interpretation is a question of law, appellate judges need not defer to the trial judge's interpretation. The appellate court can disregard the lower court's interpretation entirely.

There is a difference, however, between interpreting a statute and deciding facts that bear on the application of the statute. A legal issue, for example, might question whether the statute applied to hunting. That is a general legal question for the judge. But a fact issue might concern whether the injured visitor to the land was actually a hunter protected by the statute. The jury would decide whether the visitor was on the property for hunting or for some other purpose not of a recreational nature.

## E. DUTY IN A NEGLIGENCE CASE IS AN ISSUE OF LAW

**CASE 28. The altercation at the roller coaster: The judge, not the jury, decides whether the defendant owed a duty of care to the plaintiff.** In the following case, the dispute was over the duty of care. A youth was injured in an attack by a group of youths at an amusement park. The youth sued the amusement park on the theory that the amusement park had breached its duty to protect him from such attacks. The amusement park argued that it had no such duty and moved for summary judgment. The trial court denied the motion, and the amusement park appealed.

An actor ordinarily has a duty to exercise reasonable care when the actor's conduct could foreseeably create a risk of physical harm to another. A court may, for particular policy or precedential reasons, declare that there is no duty of reasonable care. It is the court, and not the jury, that rules whether a duty does or does not exist.

The dispute between the parties in this case was over the amusement park's duty to protect this particular patron from the physical attack that occurred on the amusement park's property. The appellate issue was whether the trial court erred in finding no duty in this case.

---

**ANTHONY R. SCOTTI, plaintiff, v. W.M. AMUSEMENTS, INC., defendant.**
640 N.Y.Supp.2d 617 (2d Dep't 1996)

**The Court:** The defendant W.M. Amusements contends that the trial court erred in denying its motion for summary judgment because it could not have reasonably anticipated or prevented the assault on plaintiff Anthony R. Scotti which took place at its amusement park. We agree.

As a general rule, a landowner must exercise reasonable care to protect patrons on its property, which includes the duty to control the conduct of third persons on their premises when they have the opportunity to control such persons and are reasonably aware of the need for such control. However, the landlord or owner of a public establishment has no duty to protect patrons against unforeseeable and unexpected assaults.

In the case before us, the record reveals that Scotti was confronted by a group of youths who had just left the amusement park's roller coaster ride, and that one member of the group moved directly in front of Scotti. Scotti admittedly responded by laughing and telling this youth, "Don't think about it. You're just a kid." Another member of the group then struck Scotti, and an altercation ensued.

According to Scotti, only seconds elapsed between the time that he first noticed the group of youths and the commencement of the altercation. Although Scotti theorizes that the operator of the roller coaster may have called Scotti over to help eject the youths from the roller coaster, there is no evidence in the record to demonstrate that the assault upon Scotti was anything other than spontaneous and unexpected. Under these circumstances, W.M. Amusements could not reasonably have been expected to anticipate or prevent the assault, and its motion for summary judgment should have been granted.

---

### ANALYSIS

The court restated the appellate question in the first sentence of the opinion. It stated that the amusement park "contends that the trial court erred in denying defendant's motion for summary judgment because it could not have reasonably anticipated or prevented the assault on plaintiff. . . ."

The dispute before the appellate court was whether the facts of the case triggered a duty of care. A common law duty of reasonable care would have been triggered only if the amusement park knew or should have known of the actual risk to Scotti. The plaintiff had the burden of presenting a prima facie case such that a jury could find that the landowner knew or should have known. Scotti failed to do so. In the face of Scotti's failure of proof, both the trial court and the appellate court ruled that, as a matter of law, the amusement park had no duty of reasonable care. The appellate issue on Scotti's appeal might have been stated as follows:

> Did the trial court err when it ruled that plaintiff Scotti failed to establish a duty of reasonable care?

or

> Did the trial court err when it ruled that plaintiff Scotti did not present a triable issue on whether the amusement park could have reasonably anticipated and prevented the assault on plaintiff?

This appellate opinion also demonstrates the usefulness of a theory of the case/IRAC analysis. The plaintiff's theory of the case was that the defendant landowner W.M. Amusements was negligent in that it should have reasonably anticipated the attack, but, by failing to do so, caused plaintiff's injury. The Issue was set out in the first paragraph as the appellate issue: Did plaintiff Scotti present sufficient evidence to establish that the defendant should reasonably have anticipated the attack? The Rule that the court applied to answer this question was a standard; a duty to prevent the risk of attack depended on whether the landowner had actual or constructive knowledge of the risk of the attack. The Analysis, found in the third and fourth paragraphs of the opinion, evaluated the plaintiff's proof and found that it insufficiently supported the inference that the defendant had or should have had such knowledge. The court's Conclusion, based on the analysis, is set forth in the last sentence of the opinion.

# CHAPTER 10

# The Holding of the Case

The holding of the case is the appellate court's answer to an appellate question. The following cases show the relationship between the appellate question and the holding.

## A. THE HOLDING OF THE CASE IS THE ANSWER THE APPELLATE COURT GIVES TO THE APPELLATE ISSUE BEFORE IT

**CASE 29. The golfer who tripped on rustic stairs: A holding cannot be broader than the appellate issue to which it is an answer.** A woman golfer tripped on a country club staircase, fell, and was injured. Her theory of the case was that the stairs, constructed with railroad ties, were unreasonably dangerous. A jury, after a full trial, found the country club was not negligent. The golfer moved to set aside the jury's verdict, but the trial court denied the motion, and the golfer appealed. The dispute on appeal was whether the jury's verdict could be reasonably supported by the evidence. The golfer also raised a separate legal issue, arguing that the trial judge erroneously allowed the jury to consider testimony concerning the absence of prior accidents. The two appellate questions might be phrased as follows:

> Did the trial court err when it declined to set aside the jury's verdict as against the weight of the evidence?

and

> Did the trial court err when it instructed the jury that it could consider the accident-free history of the steps on which the plaintiff tripped?

## MARY E. ZEIGLER, plaintiff, v. WOLFERT'S ROOST COUNTRY CLUB, defendant.

737 N.Y.Supp.2d 676 (3rd Dep't 2002)

**The Court:** Plaintiff Mary E. Zeigler brought this action to recover for injuries sustained when she fell on May 21, 1997, while descending a set of stairs on the golf course at the defendant country club in the City of Albany. Zeigler testified that her foot became lodged in a notch in one of the railroad ties used to construct the steps, causing her to fall. The testimony at trial revealed that in the more than three years that the stairs had been in use, the country club had never received any complaint regarding their condition, nor had any other fall or injury been reported in connection with the stairs.

Both Zeigler and her golfing partner testified that each of them had used these steps on numerous occasions without injury, and they had ascended those steps earlier that day without incident. The country club presented statistical data pertaining to the use of these steps revealing that prior to Zeigler's accident, thousands of people had used them without incident. Zeigler offered the testimony of an expert opining that the steps were unreasonably dangerous.

After trial, a jury rendered a verdict finding that the country club was not negligent, and the court granted judgment in the country club's favor. Thereafter, the trial judge denied plaintiff Zeigler's motion to set aside the verdict as against the weight of the evidence, finding that "a reasonable view of the evidence on the issue of negligence would support the jury's verdict in this case." Plaintiff Zeigler appeals, and we affirm the trial court's denial of Zeigler's motion.

The standard to be employed on a motion to set aside a verdict is whether the evidence so preponderated in favor of the movant that the verdict could not have been reached on any fair interpretation of the evidence. Considerable deference is to be accorded to the jury's resolution of credibility issues, including those created by conflicting expert opinions. Given the ample record of evidence on the condition of the steps, the lack of any prior reported accidents and the rather conclusory nature of the testimony of plaintiff Zeigler's expert, the jury's verdict was, in our view, based upon a fair and reasonable interpretation of the evidence.

We also reject plaintiff Zeigler's claim that the trial judge erred in instructing the jury that proof demonstrating the absence of prior accidents on the steps could be considered as evidence that the stairs were not dangerous. It is well settled that evidence of the absence of prior accidents is admissible, provided the court charges that such evidence is only a factor for consideration and not conclusive. Here, the trial court judge instructed the jury that "such evidence is not in any way conclusive on the issue of the nature or condition of the stairway." We therefore discern no error in the court's charge to the jury.

[The court affirmed the trial judge's decision to let the jury's decision in favor of the country club stand.]

**ANALYSIS**

Mary Zeigler challenged the judge's ruling denying her motion to set aside the jury's verdict. This is an appropriate legal issue for the appellate court to decide. Her second challenge involved the judge's ruling on the admissibility of testimony that no one else during the past three years had fallen; this is also an appropriate appellate legal issue.

To appreciate the holding on the admissibility of the testimony that other people had not fallen using the golf club's stairs, it is necessary to work through the entire opinion. The golfer's theory of the case was that the golf club's steps were unreasonably dangerous due to their design and construction. The country club, in its defense, offered evidence that there had not been any previous accidents in the three years that the stairs existed. This evidence offered by the county club tended to support the inference that the steps, either in their design or construction, were not unreasonably dangerous. The golfer objected to the admissibility of the testimony of the lack of accidents. The judge, however, ruled that the jury could hear the evidence of the absence of prior accidents, but not treat the absence of accidents as conclusive on the issue of dangerousness.

The holding of the case on appeal was that the trial court did not err in allowing the jury to hear the testimony on the absence of prior accidents as some evidence of the reasonableness of the stair's design.

Why is all this important? Because by working your way through the theory of the case, the evidence at trial, the legal question on appeal, and the answer given by the appellate court (the holding), you will be able to cite the opinion properly in a later case.

For example, suppose you had a client who tripped while descending a balcony aisle at a theater that had been in existence for 75 years, and the theater owner testified that no one over the previous 75 years had tripped in that aisle. Would the *Zeigler v. Wolfert's Roost Country Club* holding be relevant to whether the theater owner could use testimony of the 75 years of no accidents? The answer is probably yes.

But what if your client tripped, not on the steepness of the aisle but on a torn carpet in the aisle? That seems different, and it is. Seventy-five years of no accidents would not be relevant if the plaintiff's theory of the case was that the condition of the aisle on the day of the accident was defective due to a torn carpet.

## B. THE APPELLATE COURT'S REASONING IS INTEGRAL TO THE HOLDING OF THE CASE

**CASE 30. The pit bull at the birthday party: The appellate court's reasoning is part of the holding of the case.** In this case one of the guests at a children's birthday party brought a six-month-old pit bull to the party and

tied up the pit bull in the backyard near where the children at the party were playing. When a child at the birthday party attempted to pet the pit bull, the pit bull bit the child. The child sued the host of the birthday party on the theory that the host was negligent in allowing a guest's pit bull to remain near where the children were playing.

The dispute between the parties concerned the sufficiency of the child's evidence of the host's negligence. The plaintiff argued that it had produced a prima facie case that the host was negligent, while the host argued that the plaintiff had not produced a prima facie case. The court ruled in favor of the host. The issue on appeal was whether the judge erred in ruling that the plaintiff failed to produce a prima facie case.

**SIMEON E. MOORHEAD, plaintiff, v. MORDISTINE ALEXANDER, defendant.**
813 N.Y.Supp.2d 83 (1st Dep't 2006)

**The Court:** Evidence that defendant Mordistine Alexander permitted a guest's dog to remain on his property during a birthday party attended by young children, even after the dog, a six-month-old pit bull, began to bark constantly as children played near him and showed other signs of becoming aggressive, raises an issue of fact as to whether Alexander was negligent in maintaining his property in a reasonably safe condition.

It is for the jury to decide whether Alexander did maintain his property in a reasonably safe condition by having the dog tied up under the deck in the backyard and repeatedly announcing to his guests to stay away from the dog. It is also for the jury to decide whether any negligence on his part was superseded by plaintiff's mother's alleged negligence in allowing the infant plaintiff to pet the dog.

### ANALYSIS

The plaintiff's theory of the case was that the host was negligent in that he knew of the unreasonably dangerous condition on his property (the barking pit bull) but failed to take reasonable steps to prevent the dog from injuring the plaintiff. The trial court dismissed the case, and the injured child's lawyer appealed.

The appellate issue was: did the trial court err when it ruled that the child had failed to establish a prima facie case of negligence? The holding of the appellate court opinion was the response to that question (i.e., the trial court did err). The appellate court's reasoning supporting its holding is found in its discussion of the child's proof of the host's prior knowledge that the pit bull was becoming aggressive and dangerous: the constant barking of the pit bull, the host's own warning to the children, and other signs indicated but not listed in the appellate opinion.

The appellate issue restricted the holding of this case solely to the trial court's evaluation of the plaintiff's evidence. Essential to that holding, however, was the appellate court's reasoning. The appellate court's reasoning highlighted the constant barking of the dog. Because that fact was cited as material to the issue of the host's knowledge, the holding of the case includes the proposition that "constant barking" might be relevant in future cases where knowledge of a dog's vicious propensity is a fact issue.

Note, however, that the appellate court did not rely on the dog's breed, a pit bull. The breed, while explicitly identified, did not figure in the appellate court's reasoning and clearly was not in itself sufficient to support a prima facie case on the host's knowledge of the dog's vicious propensity.

A proper statement of the holding of this case would therefore include constant barking among the facts that might be sufficient to alert a host to a dog's aggressiveness, but not the identification of the particular breed.

# CHAPTER 11

# Taking Torts Exams

## A. WHAT DOES A TORTS ESSAY EXAM LOOK LIKE TO A STUDENT?

In *One L*, Scott Turow's book on his first year at Harvard Law School, Turow described the essay exam question he was given in torts at the end of his first term as follows:

> The first [question] was a straight issue spotter. An M.D. had given a patient a drug still in experimental stages and the series of disasters you come to expect in a Torts course had followed: blindness, car crashes, paralysis—the world, in general falling apart. We were asked what torts had occurred. (p.168)

This is a typical exam: many actors cause disastrous injuries to multiple victims in an astonishingly unexpected cascade of spreading coincidences. Such an expansive question cannot be answered by memorized information repeated back. Instead, you have to establish, on the spot, a sound legal analysis to answer the question what torts had occurred and why. The facts and circumstances set out in the question's narrative were new to Turow and to the other students taking this exam. In effect, the question replicated, in an exam context, the real-world situation in which a client walks into a lawyer's office, describes his or her injuries, and seeks advice.

Your first problem in answering the exam question is to organize the facts into a format facilitating a legal analysis. Some facts in the exam question may be presented in chronological order, other facts are scattered throughout the narrative, and others are added at the end or in a digression within the narrative. Some facts jump out as seemingly very important but may prove to be utterly irrelevant to a legal analysis. Other facts will appear to be irrelevant but may, on reflection, become central to your analysis.

The starting point to arrive at a cogent and responsive answer begins with a theory of the case. In Scott Turow's exam, for example, you might convert the narrative into a medical malpractice claim involving the lack of informed consent. The theory of the case would then be something like this: the M.D. committed medical malpractice when the M.D. prescribed a drug still in the experimental stage without either first informing the patient of the nature of the drug or obtaining the patient's informed consent, the failure of which caused the patient's injury. Having picked medical malpractice as the theory, you can identify what is required for the plaintiff to establish a prima facie case, and you can spot the key factual or legal challenges raised by the theory.

For a lack of informed consent theory to be viable, the injured patient would have to establish the appropriate standard of care, lack of consent by the patient, and that the experimental drug actually caused the patient's injuries. The first issue is a legal issue: what is the appropriate standard of care, a patient standard of care (what a patient might reasonably want to know) or a professional standard of care (what a medical professional would reasonably inform the patient).

The second issue is factual and analytical: whether the facts recited in the exam question would reasonably support a factual finding that the M.D. did not conform to the appropriate standard of care, and as a result, the patient did not make an informed consent. Consent, or lack of consent, is generally proved by circumstantial evidence. To write a good answer you will have to re-read the facts to identify which facts in the exam question will or will not support the inference of lack of consent.

The third issue is causation: will the facts support a conclusion that, had the patient been properly informed, the patient would not have consented to taking the experimental drug.

By following a theory of the case/IRAC analysis, the student is guided into reading the exam question for facts relevant to the specific issue being analyzed. You may not pick the best theory immediately, but you should try one and see how it fits the facts and whether it produces a good and legally sound result. If a theory does not look promising, explain why and try another. For most essay exams there will be many possible theories. In Scott Turow's exam question, an equally strong theory may be that the M.D. committed the tort of battery, or that the patient may also have a products liability claim against the manufacturer of the experimental drug. With each new theory additional factual and legal issues emerge. The ability to see and analyze a wide array of possible theories and issues is precisely what the essay exam is designed to test.

Issue spotting is neither magic nor an isolated action. It is a technique for asking a series of relevant questions designed to test the viability of your theories of the case against the facts you are given.

In developing your full answer, you should address as many issues as can be identified. Some of the issues may be weighted to the factual, such as whether the patient in fact consented to the experimental drug. Other issues may be weighted to the legal, such as whether the M.D. had a common law duty to disclose the experimental nature of the drug. Whatever the issue, a successful technique revolves around the principles set out in *JumpStart Torts*: theory of the case, prima facie case, burden, fact issues, and the standards for a motion for summary judgment or to dismiss the complaint.

## B. WHAT DOES AN ANSWER TO A TORTS ESSAY EXAM LOOK LIKE TO A PROFESSOR?

The work of grading essay exams is demanding, time consuming, and challenging. It is not unusual for a professor to grade only 10 or 15 essay exams a day, which means that for a torts class of 100 or more students, the grading can take more than a week. For consistency most professors develop some sort of grading sheet or rubric that identifies and organizes the array of issues students should cover in their answers. A rubric would most likely follow the identical pattern that the student should use to analyze the question: the theory of the case, issue, principle, analysis, and conclusion. The professor awards points for each element addressed by the student. The student should identify each appropriate theory of the case, spot the issues associated with that theory, bring to bear appropriate principles of tort law, and analyze all of the issues identified to their logical conclusions.

Take a careful look at the rubric for the sample question that follows. The first thing you should notice is that the rubric sets out the likely theories and breaks down those theories into each element and issue. A rubric like this puts a premium on the identification by the student of as many potential theories and related issues as can reasonably be supported by the facts. In each cell of the rubric, the law student will earn points for identifying the issue in play under a particular theory. If you miss a theory altogether or fail to see an issue that arises out of that theory, you will miss the associated points. It is therefore important to spell out in your answer all of the elements and issues that emerge from your theory or theories of the case. Do not get carried away with the splendor of the first theory or issue because you think it is the richest or most decisive, and neglect to mention the others.

No professor expects a student to spot all the issues or provide all the analyses indicated on the rubric; the exam time is too short. By setting out all the possible responses, however, the professor can systematically measure each student's answer against a consistent standard, and then, with fairness, arrange the resulting point totals along a grading curve.

Professors grading exams are not likely to study your exam answers excessively. They need to understand your answer in the first reading, which puts a premium on a clear, logical presentation. The professor has already written an answer in the form of a rubric, so the closer you adhere to that expected logic, the higher the point total is likely to be. There is obvious subjectivity in grading essay answers. The clearer the writing and more cogent the logic, the higher will be the grade.

Following this section is a sample essay question actually used in a torts exam, a rubric used to grade that exam, and two sample answers adapted from answers actually turned in. The first answer is stronger, the second weaker. Both of the student answers indicate substantial knowledge, and both passed. Note, however, how well organized the stronger answer is compared to the weaker answer, and how much easier it is to follow. The stronger answer also followed more closely the grading rubric, and therefore identified more issues, brought to bear more legal principles, and analyzed more successfully the facts of the case.

## C. SAMPLE ESSAY EXAM QUESTION

New York Crane operates large construction cranes in New York City. On December 9, 2008, New York Crane was operating a large construction crane as part of the construction of a new 41-story apartment house on East 51st Street, Manhattan.

The new building had reached 30 stories of the projected 41 stories. On the day of the collapse, as New York Crane raised a heavy load, a steel belt attaching the crane to the side of the building somehow came undone. The crane with its heavy load tottered for a moment and then fell away from the new building, striking an occupied apartment house across East 51st Street. The falling crane smashed apartment walls and balconies and sent debris flying.

Joan Smith lived in the apartment house across the street from the construction site. She was walking her dog on East 49th Street, two blocks from the construction site, when she heard the crane crash. Believing that her school-age daughter was home in her apartment, Joan became extremely anxious. In fact her daughter was still at school. When Joan arrived at her apartment, she discovered that the crane had smashed through the exterior wall of her apartment, damaged precious, irreplaceable heirlooms given to her by her grandmother, and destroyed everything in her living room, including her plasma television. She became distraught at what might have happened had she and her daughter been home. As a result she required a year of psychotherapy, could not sleep, and was so upset that she moved to a solid, one-story brick house surrounded by rosebushes in the suburbs.

Sam Jones was taking a shower in his apartment when the crane fell. His apartment was on the 14th floor, two stories below Joan Smith's apartment, but Sam's apartment escaped physical damage. On September 11, 2001, however, Sam had been a witness to the collapse of the World Trade Center and had suffered severe emotional distress following that event. With the World Trade Center in mind, Sam leaped from his shower, and, wearing nothing but his maroon monogrammed towel, ran to the interior fire stairs and rushed down the

14 flights of stairs to the street. As he bounded down the stairs Sam slipped on a wobbly tread between the 13th and 12th floors, fell, and broke his arm.

The super for Owners Corp., the corporation that owned Sam and Joan's apartment building, had known about the wobbly stair for at least six months and had ordered a repair two weeks earlier, but nothing had been done. As a result of his experience Sam's nightmares returned, he could not work for several months, and he had to return to therapy.

*The New York Times*, in its front-page article the next day, quoted the owner of New York Crane as stating that his well-trained operators followed all procedures and guidance documents and that he did not know what caused the crane to fall.

An inspector from the New York City Department of Buildings said that he was investigating but could not speculate about the accident except to say that the collapse appeared to have started when the steel strap came undone.

Joan Smith and Sam Jones consulted your law firm as to possible lawsuits.

In your interview with Sam he told you, confidentially, that his bare feet may still have been wet from the shower when he fell on the wobbly stair.

Upon being retained, the senior partner of your law firm asked your advice on all possible claims that Joan and Sam could make against any defendant. In making the assignment, she said that she understood that not all of the facts could be known at this time, but she wanted you to evaluate all possible claims that might possibly arise from the facts as known so far. What would you advise?

## D. SAMPLE ESSAY EXAM RUBRIC

| CAUSES OF ACTION | ISSUE | PRINCIPLE | ANALYSIS |
|---|---|---|---|
| **JOAN v. NEW YORK CRANE** | | | |
| **Joan's First Cause of Action: Property Damage** | | | |
| *Theory of case*: New York Crane was negligent in that it allowed the crane to fall, which caused Joan's physical damage | | | |
| *Standard of care:* Reasonable care | | | |
| *Proof of breach:* res ipsa loquitur | | | |
| *Causation:* "But for" | | | |
| *Proximate cause:* Not an issue | | | |
| *Damages:*<br>(1) Value of physical objects<br>(2) Emotional distress caused by injury to physical objects | | | |
| *Duty:*<br>(1) Duty limited to physical objects<br>(2) No duty with respect to emotional distress caused by injury to physical objects | | | |
| **Joan's Second Cause of Action: Emotional Distress** | | | |
| *Theory of the case:* New York Crane was negligent in that it allowed the crane to fall, which caused Joan's emotional distress | | | |
| *Standard of care*: Reasonable care | | | |
| *Proof of breach*: res ipsa loquitur | | | |
| *Causation:* "But for" | | | |
| *Proximate cause:* Foreseeable victim and type of injury | | | |
| *Damages:*<br>(1) Emotional distress as a result of fear for own safety<br>(2) Emotional distress at fear for safety of daughter | | | |
| *Duty:* Was Joan in the zone of danger? Fact issue | | | |

| CAUSES OF ACTION | ISSUE | PRINCIPLE | ANALYSIS |
|---|---|---|---|
| **Duty:** Was Joan in the zone of danger and witness to the injury to a family member? No—failure of proof | | | |
| **SAM v. NEW YORK CRANE** | | | |
| **Sam's First Cause of Action: Emotional Distress** | | | |
| *Theory of the case*: New York Crane was negligent in that it allowed the crane to fall on Sam's building, which caused Sam's emotional distress | | | |
| **Standard of care:** Reasonable care | | | |
| **Proof of breach:** res ipsa loquitur | | | |
| **Causation:** "But for"—Take your victim as you find him | | | |
| **Proximate cause:** Foreseeability as to the type of injury | | | |
| **Damages:** Emotional distress | | | |
| **Duty:** Was Sam in the zone of danger? Fact issue | | | |
| **Sam's Second Cause of Action: Broken Arm** | | | |
| *Theory of the case*: New York Crane was negligent in that it negligently allowed the crane to fall on Sam's building which caused Sam's broken arm | | | |
| **Standard of care:** Reasonable care | | | |
| **Proof of breach:** *res ipsa loquitur* | | | |
| **Causation:** "But for" crane accident Sam would not have run down the stairs | | | |
| **Proximate cause:** Was it foreseeable that Sam would seek to escape by fire stairs? Did Sam's injury result from the situation that the defendant's negligence created? | | | |
| **Damages:** Broken arm plus pain and suffering | | | |
| **Duty:** Runs to anyone who might be injured as a result of a falling crane | | | |

| CAUSES OF ACTION | ISSUE | PRINCIPLE | ANALYSIS |
|---|---|---|---|
| **SAM v. OWNERS CORP.** | | | |
| **Sam's Cause of Action: Broken Arm** | | | |
| *Theory of case*: Owners Corp. was negligent in that it failed to repair the fire stairs that caused Sam's injuries | | | |
| **Standard of care:** Reasonable care | | | |
| **Proof of breach:** Owners Corp. knew of the dangerous defect and did not take reasonable steps to repair | | | |
| **Causation:** "But for" the wobbly step | | | |
| **Proximate cause:** Not an issue | | | |
| **Damages:** Broken arm and related pain and suffering | | | |
| **Damages:** Severe mental distress from initial collapse of crane? | | | |
| **Duty:** Premises owner's reasonable care or standard of care based on status of invitee | | | |
| **General Issues** | | | |
| Vicarious liability | | | |
| Individual liability of employees (i.e., crane operator or building superintendent) | | | |
| Comparative negligence | | | |

## E. SAMPLE ESSAY EXAM ANSWERS

GRADER'S COMMENTS

### SAMPLE ANSWER ONE—STRONGER[*]

Joan may bring a negligence claim against New York Crane. Her theory is that New York Crane was negligent in that it committed some act (such as tampering or improper attachment or repair) that weakened the attachment of the steel belt to the building, causing the crane to come loose and fall into her apartment, which caused her property damage and resultant emotional harm.[1]

**1.** Student makes it clear that there are two types of injuries.

**2.** The organization throughout the answer is logical and in fact closely tracks the rubric that the professor had prepared.

Duty:[2] Joan will argue that New York Crane had a duty to protect her, a plaintiff located within the scope of the reasonably foreseeable risks created by New York Crane's negligence, from unreasonable risks of harm. Because her apartment was located only across the street from a large, heavy-duty crane attached to a high-rise, this element is satisfied.

Breach: Joan will argue that New York Crane breached its duty through its negligent attachment, repair, or tampering with the belt. However, because New York Crane has stated that its operators were well-trained, and that they followed all procedures and guidance documents, it may be difficult to prove what precise act by New York Crane fell below the standard of care that it owed to Joan. She will likely need to rely on the doctrine of *res ipsa loquitur* to prove breach. This doctrine allows a plaintiff to survive a motion for summary judgment by using circumstantial proof to show breach, logically eliminating other possible causes.

The first element of this doctrine is that the accident must be of the type that does not ordinarily occur without the negligence of *someone*. This element is likely satisfied because cranes do not normally just fall off high-rise buildings that they are designed to be attached to without some kind of tampering, faulty maintenance, or product defect. This element will not likely be disputed.

The next element is that the instrumentality of the accident (the faulty belt) must have been under the exclusive control of New York Crane at the time of the accident. Joan will likely argue that the crane had been in New York Crane's exclusive possession during the period leading up to the accident and, more likely than not, some negligent act of New York Crane was responsible for the accident. The fact that the crane was used

_____
*Exam has been reproduced but not edited. Comments are the author's.

by a limited number of people (the record does not indicate that anyone other than New York Crane's employees had access to the crane) coupled with its location on a dangerous and hard to access high-rise, allow a reasonable inference that, more likely than not, it was within New York Crane's exclusive control at the time of the accident. Joan can support her claim with the case of the flour barrel that fell and injured a pedestrian walking near a flour warehouse. Although no one actually saw the event as it happened, the court ruled that because it can reasonably be inferred that the barrels were under the defendant's control because of their location *inside* the warehouse, an inference that some negligence of the defendant's employees caused the barrel to fall was reasonable. In Joan's case, the location of the crane and steel belt was similar to that of the barrels, allowing a parallel inference of exclusive control (i.e., inaccessibly located within a complicated construction device, attached to a high-rise, within a construction site).[3]

The defense[4] may argue that an inference of exclusive control is unreasonable because another cause, such as a manufacturing defect, could have been responsible for the falling crane. Joan can counter, however, that it is not necessary to eliminate all other causes, only to show that they are less likely. Here New York Crane had overreaching control of the crane's operation, even if the cause possibly could have been a defect from another source. Therefore, Joan can likely establish New York Crane's breach.

The next element is causation. Joan must first show that, but for New York Crane's negligence, she would not have sustained damage to her property. This is not likely to be disputed, as the falling crane caused the damage.[5]

Also, the issue of proximate cause is not likely to be disputed. It is a normal and foreseeable consequence of the situation created by negligent attachment of a crane to a high-rise that it would fall and injure nearby property. People frequently keep priceless family heirlooms in their apartment, also.

New York Crane will likely concentrate its defense on the issue of the causal connection between the alleged negligence and Joan's damages. The fact that Joan sustained property damage is not in dispute. What is in dispute is the source of Joan's alleged emotional distress.[6] New York Crane will likely attempt to argue that the true source of this distress is Joan's overpowering fear at the time of injury that her daughter was in the apartment.

**3.** Citing cases from the casebook is not necessarily required or advised because it is so easy to make a mistake in the citation of the case. But if a case is cited, the student should explain why the case is relevant and bears on the issue discussed, just as this student did.

**4.** The defendant's response may be placed directly after the plaintiff's argument or may be grouped at the end of the plaintiff's entire argument. Here the writer has placed it immediately following the discussion of the plaintiff's position on one element and not waited to the end of the plaintiff's case. This works just fine because the argument concerning *res ipsa* stands alone. Generally, it is better to set out the plaintiff's case fully and then set out the defendant's entire response. In that way the reader sees the entire picture and is not subjected to what can become an incomprehensible back-and-forth argument. That type of "tennis match" argument is extremely hard to follow for most readers.

**5.** When a conclusion is so certain, it is best to say so, and not spin out illogical possibilities. The student here, by stating that it is not likely to be disputed, demonstrates a sense of judgment and confidence in the conclusion.

**6.** Here the student sees issues related to recovery for emotional distress but fails to spell out accurately the principles applicable to Joan's claim. A better answer would have discussed and compared a claim for emotional distress as it related to different causes: emotional distress caused by destroyed personal property, the potential injury of a daughter, and by personally being in the zone of danger.

**7.** The student gets close to an appropriate legal result, but the answer is weak because it does not sort out the various principles associated with duty when the injury is only emotional distress. The answer would be clearer and worth more if those principles had been set out. The logic is not so evident in the way the student wrote this paragraph.

**8.** It is not necessary to repeat what has already been discussed with respect to an earlier theory. But it is important to indicate what is precisely the same and what is not precisely the same.

**9.** It is acceptable to cite back to a prior discussion if exactly on point. Here the student shows an awareness of what is the same (breach and causation) and what is different (duty).

Because this turned out not to be true, New York Crane will likely argue that there is no duty or care with respect to a person's feelings about personal property. As for Joan's overwhelming fear that her daughter was in the apartment at the time of the accident, there is a question as to whether Joan may make out a prima facie case because she arguably was not in the zone of danger and her daughter absolutely was not either.[7]

Therefore, Joan likely has a negligence case against New York Crane for property damage but not for emotional distress.

Sam's theory of the case against New York Crane is that it was negligent (in the same way described by Joan's theory above[8]) and that this caused him to break his arm when he fled down the stairs in fear of the falling crane.

Sam can establish the elements of breach and causation in the same way as Joan's negligence theory against New York Crane above. He must also argue that New York Crane had a duty running to him, and that it is liable for his emotional injuries.[9]

Duty: The foreseeable risks of disaster to nearby apartments and their residents, created by New York Crane's negligence (explained above), establish that New York Crane had a duty running to Sam to protect him from unreasonable physical and emotional harm resulting from its negligent act regarding the condition of the crane.

Injury: New York Crane will be held liable for any injury that is found to be proximately caused by its negligence. The general rule is that any emotional injuries flowing from a physical injury are imputable to the tort-feasor. The question is whether New York Crane may be held liable for Sam's emotional injuries that were caused and exacerbated by its negligent use of its crane. Although the courts originally held that emotional injuries that did not flow from a physical injury were not recoverable in negligence, this rule was relaxed to allow recovery for emotional injuries sustained as a result of the defendant's negligence that creates a physical risk to the plaintiff, even if the plaintiff is not ultimately injured. To recover, many courts have ruled that the plaintiff had to have been in the "zone of danger" at the time of the accident. Because Sam was in the building into which the crane crashed, and because there was a high chance that his apartment would be hit (i.e., it was miraculously untouched), he likely fell into the zone of danger requirement.

The next issue regarding Sam's injury is whether his emotional injury is recoverable, which in large part may have resulted from the exacerbation of his preexisting fear of terrorist attack. Under the eggshell plaintiff rule, however, a plaintiff is allowed to recover from any ancillary emotional or physical harm caused by the defendant's negligence, no matter how unexpected it may have been. Sam should argue that his case is like a diabetic who was involved in a minor accident in which he sustained a minor finger injury. Because of his prior condition, he got gangrene and the finger had to be amputated. He was allowed to recover.

Sam may also argue that his whole experience, including his broken arm, was connected to New York Crane's negligence, and therefore that his emotional injuries are interconnected to the physical injury that resulted from this negligence. New York Crane has its strongest case here. However, Sam can make a good policy argument that the goals of Tort law include deterrence and compensation in proper proportion to a defendant's conduct. Sam should argue that it would violate this principle to allow a defendant whose negligence has directly caused serious emotional injury (i.e., Sam has recurring nightmares, could not work for months, and needed therapy) to escape liability, simply because it is unclear to what extent the injury was occasioned by a physical injury.[10]

**10.** By focusing on the injury, the student demonstrated an ability to handle complexity. The nature of the injured raised serious issues of duty, causation, and proximate causation.

New York Crane may also argue that its negligence did not cause Sam's broken arm, but that the intervening negligence by Owner's Corp. was the sole cause or, alternatively, an intervening event that cut off its liability.

Sam would respond that it is foreseeable that, when a crane negligently falls, a person in the zone or in danger, would attempt to flee, and that escaping by the fire stairs is a foreseeable event. Sam would argue that his broken arm was the product of the situation created by the negligence of New York Crane. This should be enough to create a fact issue on the liability of New York Crane for Sam's broken arm as well as his emotional distress.[11]

**11.** This answer demonstrates that the student understands that the question did not call for a final verdict, but only whether a prima facie case could be established, and that required at a minimum that there be fact issues with respect to material issues.

Sam's theory of the case against his landlord (Owner's Corp.) is that it was negligent in that it failed to take reasonably prompt steps to repair its stair when it had notice of the problem, and that Sam was injured when he tripped on the faulty stair as he ran down the stairs.

Duty: The landlord had a duty running to Sam to take reasonable steps to protect him against unreasonable risks of harm about which it knew. This would be true even in states following the traditional common law. Sam would be an invitee, and the stairs was a common area.[12]

Because the landlord knew of the wobbly stair six months in advance of the accident, and Sam was its tenant, duty is established.

Breach: The landlord delayed repairing the wobbly stair for six months. This created a foreseeable risk that someone could be injured when running down the stairs in the face of an emergency, such as a fire.

The landlord may argue that the foreseeable risks of negligence included only injuries expected during a fire evacuation. Sam should counter, however, that the foreseeable risks created by landlord's failure to repair should be construed as including *all* reasonably foreseeable emergencies. New York City is a city constantly under construction, using heavy-duty equipment. It was not extraordinary that an emergency situation could be created by a malfunctioning piece of construction equipment, which would require quick and frantic evacuation. Therefore, breach is likely established.

Causation: More likely than not, we can say that but for the wobbly stair, Sam would not have been injured when he ran from the falling crane.

Proximate Cause: Owner's Corp. will likely argue that Sam's extreme emotional injury and loss of work ability were not normal and foreseeable consequences of the situation created by its negligent failure to repair the stair. Sam should argue that because his emotional injury was caused in part by his fall and broken arm, Owner's Corp. should not be absolved from liability simply because the crane was what caused him to run down the stairs. Sam should argue that the combination of physical pain with the emotional harm was what caused his extreme reaction. The defense may argue, however, that it is not credible that Sam could have suffered such severe emotional distress from tripping on the tread and breaking his arm. Although there is a chance that the court[13] may let the claim against Owner's Corp. for negligence go forward, there is a good possibility that the court will grant summary judgment in favor of Owner's Corp., with respect to the extreme emotional distress because that landlord's negligence was the proximate cause of Sam's emotional injuries.[14]

**12.** A better answer would have explained why Sam would be considered an invitee and how that status affected duty.

**13.** The student by this sentence indicates that the student understands how the judge's role differs from the jury's role. A more detailed discussion would have been even better.

**14.** This paragraph is somewhat confused, but it indicates that the student has spotted the issue of whether Owners Corp. should be held liable for the extreme emotional distress triggered by the original crane accident, and then made a fair attempt at analyzing the issue.

## SAMPLE ANSWER TWO—WEAKER[*]
## Joan and Sam v. New York Crane

Joan and Sam's ("P")[1] theory of the case against New York Crane ("D") is that D was negligent in that it failed to properly secure the steel belt to the crane, causing it to fall and thereby causing them to suffer severe emotional distress and physical injuries.[2]

P could argue that D had a duty running to them according to the reasonable person standard that any reasonable person in same and similar circumstance would exercise a degree of care to prevent any foreseeable harm arising from their conduct. Because in this case D claims that they exercised all reasonable procedures and followed the guidelines, P might have some trouble[3] proving how D breached their duty.[4] Therefore, P's best chance of recovery is to invoke the doctrine of *res ipsa loquitur* and show that it does not matter how the accident happened, but that it happened, and more likely than not, it was D's fault.

*Res ipsa loquitur* requires that P establish three elements such that (1) the accident is of a kind that normally does not happen without the negligence of someone, (2) that defendant had exclusive control of the instrumentality that caused the injury, and (3) that P did not cause/contribute in any way to the accident.

The first and second elements can clearly be established. A crane does not usually fall from above without the negligence of someone; that is not the normal/intended purpose of a crane. Furthermore, both Sam and Joan could not have contributed in any way to the accident. They were in no way involved in the operations of the crane.

The second element is the one most challenging to be overcome by both Ps. Exclusive control has been applied more and more flexibly in recent times by the courts. P does not have to prove that D had absolutely exclusive control but that all other possibilities are greatly reduced so that negligence falls on D. P could argue that it is more likely than not that it was the negligence of D in failing to properly secure the steel belt that caused the belt to become loose and fall. P could point to the fact that the crane had been carefully inspected

---

*Exam has been reproduced but not edited. Comments are the authors.

### GRADER'S COMMENTS

**1.** It is tempting to use abbreviations, but using abbreviations makes it harder for the reader. In this case, combining the two plaintiffs caused the student to miss issues as well.

**2.** The two plaintiffs have different theories of the case dictated by the nature of their individual injuries. This student gets off on the wrong foot by not seeing the difference between the two plaintiffs' situations.

**3.** Too conclusory a statement. The student should have spelled out what the proof problem was, not just characterized it as trouble.

**4.** The proof problem in the question is that no one knows why the crane fell, and it may be that no one will ever know.

and met the industry required standards and passed the test when it was sold to *D*. Therefore these circumstantial evidences can allow a reasonable jury to infer that it must have been some kind of negligence on *D*'s part in failing to properly secure the steel belt to the crane, because the other possible causes can be greatly reduced.

*P*s can argue that but for the negligence of *D* in failing to properly secure the crane, it would not have fallen and caused damage to their apartments,[5] also causing severe emotional and physical damage to themselves. Alternatively *P*s could argue that the negligence of *D* was a substantial cause of their injuries such that their negligence greatly increased the chance of the crane falling from the loose belt and coming down on their apartment building causing severe damage and injury to themselves.[6]

*P*s could argue that *D*'s negligence is the proximate cause of their injuries[7] because it is foreseeable that the tenants living in the apartment building across their construction site would suffer any kind of damage if they fail to properly secure the crane and if it ends up falling.[8]

*D* could counterargue *P*'s *res ipsa* claim by saying that they had taken all reasonable precautions. *D* could point to the fact that its well-trained operators followed all procedures and guidance documents, and it took all reasonable care in attaching the steel to the crane.[9] They could further argue that they did not have exclusive control of the crane because it was sold by its manufacturer and the steel belt/crane could have been defective in its design, and they had no control over the design/manufacture of the crane.[10]

*P*s would be able to recover for their severe emotional distress, loss of enjoyment of life, present/future income loss, relocation expenses, Sam's hospital/medical expenses for the present and future (for his broken arm), and loss of consortium and damage to their valuables/property.[11]

### Sam v. Owners Corp.

Sam's (*P*) theory of the case against Owners Corp. (*D*)[12] is that *D* was negligent in that it failed to maintain its premises in a safe condition, thereby causing *P* to fall on the wobbly stairs and injure himself.

As stated in *Rowland v. Christian*, a reasonable landowner owes a duty to maintain its premises in a safe condition (or to

---

**5.** Only one apartment was damaged, and the emotional distress experienced by the two plaintiffs had different sources which is highly relevant. Here the injuries suffered are blended and result in a confused answer.

**6.** No explanation as to why the student discussed an alternative proof of causation.

**7.** Lack of specificity results in an incomplete discussion.

**8.** This is a wholly inadequate discussion of proximate cause. The question called for separate proximate cause discussions concerning Sam's emotional distress injury and his physical injury. Joan's emotional distress injury should be discussed under duty but might also be discussed as a proximate cause issue.

**9.** No indication why this argument by the defendant would be relevant or how persuasive it would likely be.

**10.** Speculation. There were no facts in the question concerning design or manufacture.

**11.** Discussion of damages is conclusory and without analysis. No discussion of individual injuries. Joan had separate claims, one for property damages and the other for emotional distress. The loss of consortium is simply thrown In without any relevance to the case.

**12.** Abbreviations get quite confusing because *D* now refers to a different defendant. I would advise not using any abbreviations at all unless they are universally understood, such as U.S.A. or the I.R.S.

warn of dangers) in light of the probability of injury to those on its premises.[13] A reasonable landowner would inspect its premises and ensure that they are in a safe condition in order to protect the people on its premises from any foreseeable harm/risk arising out of any dangerous/defective condition.

D breached its duty by failing to fix the wobbly stairs he had known for six months of its dangerous condition but failed to take any reasonable measures to fix it.[14] D had even ordered repair only two weeks prior to P's accident, and when nothing had been done, D still failed to act.

But for D's failure to fix the wobbly stairs, the injury to P would not have occurred. But for the stairs being wobbly, P would not have fallen when he stepped on it, slipped, lost his balance, and fell. Alternatively it could be argued that D's negligence was a substantial cause of P's injuries such that D's failure to fix the wobbly condition of the stair greatly multiplied the chance that P would step on it, slip/lose his balance, and fall[15]

Furthermore, D's failure to fix the wobbly stairs is the proximate cause of P's physical injury of his broken arm.[16] Could D have foreseen that P would be injured by stepping on a wobbly stair and falling to the ground? P's injury is a foreseeable consequence of D's negligence. P is within the general class of people who are foreseeably exposed to the risk arising from D's negligent conduct, because P is a building tenant and uses the stairs quite often.[17] Furthermore, P's injury is the type of injury foreseeable to result from D's failure to fix the stairs, because it is not unusual for someone to step on a wobbly stair and fall and break his arm.

D could argue that although it had a duty to exercise reasonable care to the tenants who would foreseeably be injured on its premises, however, its failure to fix the wobbly stairs is not the proximate cause of P's injuries.[18]

D could argue that it was P's contributory negligence that proximately caused his injuries. He[19] could point out that normally P would not run down the stairs in the everyday course of events and that he was being negligent for his own safety by running down stairs. It is just common knowledge that running down the stairs poses any kind of risk of falling. P assumed that risk when he ran down the stairs, and since he was negligent on his own behalf, he should comparatively be liable.[20]

**13.** This is not an accurate statement of the premises owner's duty. The duty is to maintain the premises in a reasonably safe condition, not a perfectly safe condition.

**14.** No explanation why knowledge for six months is a relevant fact. If relevant, the student should have explained why.

**15.** No explanation why the student discussed alternative proofs of causation.

**16.** Proximate cause, with respect to the broken arm, is not an issue in this case. This discussion only proves the obvious.

**17.** There are no facts in the question to support this assertion. Students cannot just make up facts and add them to the question.

**18.** This conclusion does not follow from the discussion immediately above, which proves the contrary.

**19.** Pronouns may be just as confusing as abbreviations. Who is the "he" in this sentence? It is best to avoid using pronouns altogether, even if it means repeating a name two or three times in a single sentence.

**20.** Assumption of the risk is not appropriate under these circumstances. The only defense would be contributory negligence or comparative negligence.

**21.** There is no factual basis for arguing that Sam "should have known" about the wobbly stair.

**22.** This is not a persuasive argument because it is the owner's duty to maintain a reasonably safe premises.

**23.** There are no facts to support these forms of damages, and the discussion only lists the items without explaining them.

**24.** Merely suggesting a legal issue and then leaving it hanging without an analysis or explanation gets few points. It suggests that the student saw something but does not know how to handle the issue.

*D* could also argue that *P* had known of the danger of the wobbly stair since it had been in that condition for six months, or that he should have known of the danger.[21] If *P* knew the danger, then *D* could argue that it was his careless disregard of the dangerous wobbly stair that caused him to fall.[22]

Sam has a prima facie case against *D* for negligence because *D* owed him a duty and breached it, and that breach was the cause of his injuries. Sam could collect damages for his physical injuries, present and future medical costs, perhaps loss of consortium, and for his future earnings for the several months that he will be unemployed.[23] Sam could also collect for emotional distress for his nightmares, if he can show in some way that they were connected to his fall and worries about not being able to use his arm.[24]

# CHAPTER 12

# The Finish Line

*J*umpstart Torts will help make a law student a better lawyer by providing the necessary skills to do well in law school.

Lawyers use language in a special way. Lawyers reveal the level of their skills by how they use words. Lawyers do not "motion the court," they make a motion. Judges "rule" on law, while juries "find" the facts. A motion for summary judgment differs from a motion to dismiss a complaint. These and other terms have to be memorized until they become second nature.

Lawyers are regularly presented with disorganized and partial statements of facts. Facts must be organized into a theory of the case as the first step in the legal analysis.

Lawyers provide advice and legal analyses but must first identify a discrete legal issue. Once an issue relevant to a theory of the case has been identified, the lawyer can then apply the appropriate rules, standards, and principles to the facts to create a legal analysis and reach a credible conclusion.

Lawyers handling tort cases must not only know tort doctrines, they must also know the litigation processes and procedures that govern how tort cases are litigated. A theory of a case, for example, is only viable if the lawyer for the plaintiff can produce a prima facie case. To establish a prima facie case, a plaintiff can offer direct testimony but may also rely on a presumption to prove a fact, or use circumstantial evidence to infer the existence of one fact from proof of another. Ultimately, a prima facie case of a tort claim, however it is proved, must pass the procedural test of probability: could a jury find, by a preponderance of the evidence, that the plaintiff has established a prima facie case?

Lawyers read and rely on the holdings of judicial opinions. Identifying the issue addressed in a judicial opinion is the first step toward understanding and applying the holding of the opinion to other facts and situations.

These are lawyer's skills that will be used for a lifetime. *Jumpstart Torts* provides a path toward mastering these skills.

# Legal Terms
## (an alphabetical listing)

**Affidavit:** An affidavit is a formal written statement, made under oath or affirmed, given by either a party or a witness, and used to bring a fact or opinion to the attention of the judge. For example, the defendant in an auto accident lawsuit might submit an affidavit by a witness describing what the witness saw as support for the defendant's motion for summary judgment.

**Affirmative Defense:** In an affirmative defense the defendant sets out additional allegations that, if established, would affirmatively refute the plaintiff's claims. An affirmative defense is affirmative in the sense that the defendant bears the affirmative burden to allege and then to prove the defense. Examples of affirmative defenses in a negligence case include the claim that the plaintiff assumed the risk of injury or, by his or her own negligence, caused or contributed to the injury. There also may be procedural affirmative defenses such as lack of jurisdiction over the defendant, or that the plaintiff missed the deadline set by the statute of limitations for filing a complaint.

**Answer:** The answer is the defendant's formal written response to the plaintiff's complaint in which the defendant denies or admits the plaintiff's allegations of facts, and asserts any affirmative defenses he or she might have to the plaintiff's claims or causes of action.

**Appeal:** A litigant on the losing side of a ruling by the trial court judge may appeal to a higher court. Each state has its own rules governing when an appeal might be taken. In some states an appeal may only be taken at the conclusion of the trial after entry of judgment, whereas other states allow appeals to be taken prior to or during the trial. For instance, in some states an appeal may be taken after a judge has denied a party's motion for summary judgment, while other states refuse to allow the losing party on a motion for summary judgment to appeal until the entire trial is over.

**Appellant:** The appellant is the party who has appealed. Either plaintiff or defendant may appeal, so either may be called the appellant when he or she gets to the appellate court. Sometimes an appellant is called the petitioner.

**Appellate Court:** An appellate court is a court that hears appeals. Most states have two levels of appellate courts, a mid-level appellate court and a high court.

**Appellate Issue:** An appellate issue is the legal question put before the appellate court by the appellant.

**Appellee:** The appellee is the party responding to the appeal. The appellee defends the order or judgment of the trial court which is being challenged by the appellant. Sometimes an appellee is called a *respondent*.

**Breach:** The term *breach* in a negligence case indicates that the defendant's conduct did not measure up when compared to the appropriate standard of care. Breach is a conclusion rather than a factual allegation. In considering whether a breach has occurred, the jury must compare the defendant's actual conduct with what a person should have done as required by the standard of care.

**Burden of Going Forward:** The burden of going forward determines the order in which the trial proceeds. Generally the plaintiff has the burden of going forward first with the plaintiff's direct case. The defendant has the burden of going forward with evidence to support an affirmative defense, but only after the plaintiff has successfully presented the plaintiff's direct case.

**Burden of Persuasion:** The ultimate burden in the litigation is called the burden of persuasion, or, alternatively, the burden of proof. The "burden" in the term is the risk of nonpersuasion. In a tort case the burden of persuasion falls on the plaintiff who must establish by a preponderance of the evidence all of the elements necessary to sustain his or her claim. The defendant may also have a burden of persuasion when, for example, the defendant asserts an affirmative defense.

**Claim for Relief or Cause of Action:** These terms refer to the sections of the complaint in which the plaintiff sets out the plaintiff's separate theories supporting compensation. A plaintiff often alleges more than one claim for relief or cause of action. The usual practice is to separate the claims by headings such as First Claim for Relief, Second Claim for Relief, or First Cause of Action, Second Cause of Action, and so forth. Separate claims for relief or causes of action are intended to represent separate theories of the case. The term *cause of action* is sometimes used as a synonym for theory of the case.

**Common Law:** Common law is the legal system that evolved from English judge-made law. The major characteristic of common law is that it developed, and continues to develop, out of judicial decisions in individual cases rather than from statutes enacted by state legislatures. The body of English common law was received by each of the states of the United States, except Louisiana, and continues to form the basis of the law of each state. Because each state has its own version of the common law, tort law may vary from state to state.

**Common Law Tort:** A common law tort is a claim based on the breach of the common law of the state. A common law tort is distinguished from a statutory tort. A statutory tort is a claim based on the breach of a statute enacted by the state legislature.

**Comparative Negligence:** Under a comparative negligence regime (also called comparative fault), the jury allocates responsibility for the injury among the parties. Thus damages awarded the plaintiff will be reduced by the percentage of responsibility that the jury assigns to the plaintiff's own conduct. Comparative negligence has the advantage of assuring the plaintiff of some recovery even in circumstances where the plaintiff was partially responsible for his or her own injury. This method of allocating fault replaced the common law rule of contributory negligence under which the plaintiff was denied all compensation if the plaintiff's own negligence contributed to his or her injury. Different versions of comparative negligence exist among the states and vary as to whether and how the calculation is to be made.

**Complaint:** The complaint is the initial written document in a civil action that formally sets out the plaintiff's claim against the defendant. In the complaint the plaintiff identifies the defendant or defendants, sets out the facts on which the plaintiff bases his or her theory of the case, and describes the injury and amount of compensation demanded. The part of the complaint in which the plaintiff sets out the monetary demand is sometimes referred to by the Latin phrase, *ad damnun* clause. Some states prohibit plaintiffs in tort cases from stating a dollar amount in the *ad damnun* clause to prevent unrealistic multibillion dollar claims from being asserted.

**Constructive Knowledge or Constructive Notice:** These terms are synonyms and describe the circumstance where the facts in the case are sufficient for the jury to infer that the person knew or should have known, and therefore that person can be treated as if he or she in fact did know.

**Court:** The location of judicial activity, either trial or appellate. Lawyers also use the term *court* as a synonym for *judge* or *panel of judges*, as in the statement that "The court wrote in its opinion . . ." or "The court decided. . . . "

**Damages:** Damages are the monetary compensation sought by the plaintiff to compensate for the injury suffered. The terms *injury* and *damages* are not interchangeable. *Injury* refers to the actual physical or mental harm experienced by the plaintiff, while the term *damages* refers to their monetary equivalent.

**Defendant:** The person against whom the plaintiff has brought a lawsuit and from whom the plaintiff seeks compensation.

**Demurrer:** A demurrer is the older common law term for a motion by the defendant to dismiss the complaint as deficient as a matter of law.

**Deposition:** A deposition, or an examination before trial, is oral testimony given under oath, usually in a lawyer's office without a judge present. The questioning is done by each party's attorney. An oral deposition is usually transcribed, recorded, or videotaped, and has the effect of locking in a party or witness's story. Under appropriate circumstances, the testimony may be read into evidence at the trial or used to challenge a witness's trial testimony.

**Direct Case:** The direct case is either party's initial presentation of evidence at trial. A direct case is not complete until the opposing side has had an opportunity to cross examine the witnesses presented by the party offering the direct case.

**Discovery:** Discovery is the general term for court-sanctioned processes used prior to trial by which each party obtains information about the other side's claims or defenses. The term *discovery* covers a wide variety of methods. These include oral testimony under oath, physical examination by medical experts, written answers to written questions, exchanges of documents, and inspections of articles or locations. Discovery avoids surprises at trial, allows each party to assess the strength or weakness of each other's position, and encourages settlement of the claim prior to trial.

**Duty of Care:** To have a duty of care denotes that one person has a legally enforceable obligation to another, the breach of which permits the injured person to be compensated. In a negligence case, duty is a threshold issue to be decided by the judge. Whether there is a duty of care, however, cannot be analyzed without first setting out the theory of the case.

**Evidence:** Evidence consists of those testimonial statements, objects, and documents allowed to be presented in a trial court for consideration by the jury. The rules of evidence govern what testimony or documents may be allowed to be admitted into evidence during the trial. For example, witnesses may be allowed to testify as to what they actually saw themselves but may not be allowed to testify about what someone else told them they saw (hearsay).

**Fact Issue and Triable Issue:**  A fact issue is a dispute between the parties over the existence of a fact, the interpretation of a fact, or the inferences that may be drawn from a fact. Fact issues are resolved by the jury or, when there is no jury, by the judge. A triable issue is a fact issue of sufficient materiality that its resolution requires a trial.

**General Defense:**  In a general defense, defendants deny the truth of, or the legal implications of, the allegations set out by the plaintiff in the complaint.

**Holding:**  The holding is the appellate court's answer to a legal question. An appellate court affirms, reverses, or modifies the decision from the lower court.

**Inference:**  An inference is a fact not directly proved, but which is logically drawn from another fact or truth. Facts are inferred through a process of reasoning by which the fact or proposition sought to be established is deduced as a logical consequence from other facts already proved or admitted. Inferences may be strong or weak, possible or impossible, compelling or improbable. Much of the art of advocacy involves identifying and evaluating the strengths or weaknesses of inferences.

**Injury:**  Injury is the basis for a claim in tort. A physical injury refers to either bodily injury or property damage. Injuries may also include injuries to emotional well-being, reputation, pain and suffering, medical expenses, and loss of income.

**Instructions:**  At the conclusion of the evidentiary portion of the trial, the judge speaks directly to the jury and instructs the members of the jury on how they are to resolve the fact issues developed in the trial. These instructions may also be referred to as the judge's charge to the jury. Jury instructions are also sometimes given at the beginning of the case.

**IRAC:**  The acronym IRAC refers to a standard form of legal analysis useful for addressing single, discrete legal issues. The letters stand for Issue, Rule, Analysis, and Conclusion.

**Judgment:**  The judgment is the final order in a tort case that incorporates the jury's verdict and the judge's approval of the verdict. The trial of a case concludes when the trial judge orders that a judgment be entered by the clerk of the court in the court's official records. A judgment is entered irrespective of whether the plaintiff or the defendant wins. As a technical matter, a judgment is usually not final until it is actually entered by the clerk of the court.

**Jury:** The jury resolves factual disputes between the parties, including how much compensation to award the injured party. Juries usually are made up of 6 or 12 persons selected for each case from panels of persons called to jury duty. A trial jury resolves disputes by 'finding the facts.' The parties to a litigation may waive a jury and instead submit their factual disputes to the trial judge sitting without a jury, in which case the trial judge becomes the fact finder.

**Lawsuit:** A lawsuit is a commonly used nontechnical term for any civil claim filed in a court of law. A synonym is the word *action* which is usually defined as a civil law claim brought by one private party against another private party. A criminal charge is referred to as a prosecution rather than a lawsuit.

**Liability:** The term *liability* refers to the judicial finding that a party is legally answerable to another party. A plaintiff's tort claim for an injury may be divided into two phases, the liability phase and the damages phase. The liability phase determines whether the defendant is legally answerable for the injury. The damages phase determines the amount the defendant must pay the plaintiff in compensation for the injury.

**Limitations:** A statute of limitations is a legislative enactment prescribing the time within which a particular type of claim may be enforced in court. A typical statute of limitations for a negligence complaint may require that an action be commenced within three years of the injury.

**Material Fact:** A material fact is a fact that has substantial importance to the result at trial. A material fact possesses the capability of properly influencing the result of the trial.

**Motions:** Parties to a litigation bring legal issues to the judge for resolution by making a motion. For example, a defendant might move (i.e., ask the judge) to dismiss the plaintiff's complaint, or move to disqualify an expert witness. The correct usage is a party *moved* or *made a motion*, as in the defendant moved for summary judgment; never a party *motioned* the court. Motions may be written or oral, depending on the circumstances. The judge either denies or grants a motion. It is incorrect to say the judge approved, sustained, or adopted a motion.

**Motion to Dismiss the Complaint:** A motion to dismiss a complaint is a motion made by a defendant asking the trial judge to rule the plaintiff's complaint deficient as a matter of law.

**Motion to Set Aside a Verdict:**  After the jury has returned its verdict, a party may move to set aside the verdict on the grounds that the evidence could not, under any reasonable interpretation, support the verdict. This motion is also called a motion for a judgment n.o.v., an abbreviation of the Latin *non obstante veredicto*. The judge should allow the verdict to stand so long as the jury's verdict may be supported by a reasonable interpretation of the evidence.

**Movant and Nonmovant:** The movant is the party making a motion. The nonmovant is the person against whom the motion is made.

**Negligence:** A claim for negligence is a common law claim for compensation for an injury suffered by the plaintiff that was caused by the negligent conduct of the defendant. Negligent conduct is conduct that falls below the standard established by law for the protection of others against unreasonable risk of harm.

**Opinion:** A judicial opinion is a judge's formal explanation, usually written, stating the basis for the judicial decision.

**Order:** When a judge directs that something be done or not be done, that directive is called an *order*. An order can be as limited as directing a witness to appear at a deposition to answer questions, or it can affect the entire case as, for example, an order dismissing a plaintiff's complaint.

**Plaintiff:** The injured person who initiates the lawsuit and who is seeking compensation.

**Pleading:** Pleading is the general term used by the common law to describe the documents bringing an action to court. The pleadings in a case refer to the complaint and answer, as well as other filings with the court setting out a party's formal claims or defenses.

**Preponderance of the Evidence:** Preponderance of the evidence is the general standard or measure by which the jury resolves a fact issue in a tort trial. Preponderance of the evidence is usually described as evidence sufficient to make a fact more likely than not. It is not a precise measure. It allows for uncertainty because the conclusion reached by the jury need not be without doubt, only that it is supported by a preponderance of the evidence. This standard is less strict than the well-known beyond a reasonable doubt standard used in a criminal trial.

**Prima Facie:** Latin, meaning "at first sight." A prima facie case is one where the evidence is sufficiently persuasive to establish the fact asserted. A party establishes a prima facie case by producing factual evidence in support of his or her claim which is sufficient to require the opposing party to respond. A plaintiff has presented a prima facie case when it can be said that a jury, after viewing all of the evidence presented by the plaintiff, could decide in favor of the plaintiff's theory of the case. The judge, acting as gatekeeper, decides whether the plaintiff has met the burden of producing a prima facie case.

**Proximate Cause:** The term *proximate cause* describes judicially created standards to decide how broadly to extend liability for injuries resulting from an individual act of negligence. Application of the doctrine of proximate cause triggers consideration of fairness and foreseeability to limit the rippling effects of negligent conduct. Proximate cause, as a result, is a conclusion following application of the standards rather than an allegation of fact. The Restatement of Torts (Third) prefers the term *scope or liability* rather than the term *proximate cause* because the concept is one of limitations of liability rather than factual causation. Restatement of Torts (Third) Section 29.

**Remand:** A remand is an order by an appellate court sending the case back to the lower court. A remand may include additional instructions to the lower court judge as set out in the opinion of the appellate court.

**Res Ipsa Loquitur:** This is a Latin phrase for "the thing speaks for itself." It is used to describe the factual circumstances where the injury could only logically happen as a result of the negligence of the defendant.

**Restatement of Torts:** Because tort law varies from state to state, the American Law Institute, a legal reform organization of lawyers, academics, and judges, publishes a treatise on tort law with the goal of having the states bring their tort laws into greater agreement with each other and to do so by selecting the better of the various state rules available. The treatise presents its conclusions as numbered rules, with explanations and examples. There have been three restatements of torts and a separate restatement of products liability. Judges view the restatements as persuasive but not binding.

*Ruling* **versus** *Finding*: These terms are often confused. The correct usage is that legal issues are ruled upon, and facts are found. The verbs reflect the distinctive roles played by the judge, who rules on the law, and the jury, which finds the facts. Because the roles are not interchangeable, neither are the terms. *Correct*: The judge *ruled* that the complaint stated a cause of action for which relief could be granted, while the jury *found* the defendant was negligent in running the red light.

**Settlement:** A settlement is an agreement ending the litigation by consent of the parties. Most tort claims end in a settlement and are not fully tried all the way to jury verdict. Settlements have the advantage of allowing the parties to agree on the amount of compensation that must be paid rather than have the jury impose an amount.

**Standard of Care:** The standard of care is the standard against which the defendant's conduct is judged in a negligence case. The general standard of care for common law torts is what a reasonable person would do in the same or similar circumstances. The standard of care may vary as, for example, with respect to physical conditions like blindness, professional activities like medical services, or, in the case of young children, age and experience.

**Summary Judgment:** A motion for summary judgment asks the trial judge to decide the case without a trial. The motion may be made by either the plaintiff or defendant. The party making the motion seeks to convince the judge that there is no dispute concerning a material fact, and as a result, there is no need to have a trial to resolve factual disputes. The judgment is "summary" in the sense that it eliminates the fact-finding portion of the trial and allows the judge to decide the case and go straight to the entry of judgment.

**Summons:** A summons is the formal, judicially required notification to the defendant that the plaintiff has commenced an action against the defendant. The nature of the action and facts supporting the action are set out in the complaint, not the summons.

**Theory of the Case:** A theory of the case sweeps together into a single, broad statement the *factual* elements necessary to support the plaintiff's claim. To create a theory of the case, the plaintiff organizes the facts to support each of the elements the plaintiff must prove to establish his or her claim. Sometimes the term *cause of action* is used as a synonym for theory of the case.

**Tort:** The name given to a wrong or wrongful act causing injury, for which a legal claim may be made. *Black's Law Dictionary* defines a tort as "a legal wrong committed upon the person or property independent of contract." The distinction made by this definition is between tort and contract. If a person trips on a hazard in a grocery store and is injured, the wrong is a tort and the claim for compensation is made pursuant to tort law. If, by contrast, the grocery store hired the person but then refused to pay the promised salary, the wrong would be a breach of contract, and the claim for the wrongfully withheld salary would be under contract law.

**Trial Court:** The trial court is where tort cases are initially tried and where fact disputes are resolved by the jury.

**Verdict:** The verdict is the decision by the jury resolving the fact issues, including whether and how much compensation in damages the defendant should pay the plaintiff.

# Index